# LYRICA

HOP AS
FULNESS

BORN I

# DHARMA

PARALLAX PRESS
PO Box 7355
Berkeley, CA 94707
parallax.org

Parallax Press is the publishing division of
Plum Village Community of Engaged Buddhism, Inc.
© 2025 Ofosu Jones-Quartey

Cover and inteior design by Katie Eberle
Tibetan Calligraphy Artworks by Dharma Artist Tashi
Mannox: Cloud - Shodo free-brush, 17-18-19. Born of
Bindu, 20. May Goodness Increase - Shodo free-brush
with Tibetan calligraphy, 38. Garland, 46. Lingam of
single stroke Ashe, 53. Ensō, 54-55-56-57. Le Grand
Banc Ensō, 123, 125. Present Attentiveness - Shodo free-
brush with Tibetan calligraphy, 159.
Cover photo and interior photos by Erich Morse: 6, 41
Interior photos by Jeff Ray: 23, 66, 92, 157
Interior photo by Rob Walsh: 81
Interior photo by Jammie Patton: 95
Interior photo by Brother Phap Huu: 135

Printed in Canada by Friesens
Printed on recycled paper

Parallax Press's authorized representative in the EU is
SARL Boutique La Bambouseraie Point UH,
Le Pey, 24240 Thénac, France
Email: europe@parallax.org

ISBN 9780984627165
Ebook ISBN 9780984627189
Library of Congress Control Number: 2025935321

1 2 3 4 5 FRIESENS 28 27 26 25 24

# Dedica-tion

*To my wife Ayanna—the sun within my heart—
and to our children Sundara, Samadhi, Sati and Siddhattha—
the rays of the sun.*

*To my parents, teachers, and ancestors of spirit and flesh.*

*To the Buddha, Dharma, and Sangha.*

*To Hip-Hop.*

*Please accept this book as an imperfect offering.*

*I love you all.*

# contents

LYRICAL
DHARMA
PLAYLIST ▶

# Fore-word

It is hard to express

how important I feel this book is.  I wept many times, reading it, imagining the sound of music beneath the lyrics of the songs.  Actually, I had no idea what to expect, as I began to read the manuscript.  I know almost nothing about hip-hop, though a friend of mine, Quincy Jones, was an early champion of it. I love music, but as I have grown older, I find I can rarely be distracted from the sounds of wind and rain and rustling of the trees.  And yet, when Ofosu shared one of his songs with me after a retreat I was immediately moved and wanted to share it.  I could feel the energy of loving self-acceptance in it; that we are all here, in the Universe, experiencing pain, yes, but also wonder, together.  I loved that he encourages us to grow; to know our good fortune.  To be blessed with *hereness*. Like the rest of us, he has suffered.

That part of his journey too is offered, beautifully, bravely, thoughtfully, as medicine.

—ALICE WALKER

# Pre-face

Can hip-hop be contemplative art?

My music, my work as a teacher (encourager), is for anyone who experiences suffering and is working to overcome it. It is for people who are imperfectly on the path of self discovery and awakening. It's for all of us humans, for people who struggle, as I have done and continue to do. The lyrics in this book and the stories behind them are expressions of my life as a human walking on, drifting from, and returning to the path of transforming intense suffering into liberation of the mind, body, and heart, again and again. They are the stories of my life.

I've been an artist for as long as I remember—music, words, and visual arts have always been mediums I love. My love for the arts is inspired by my parents. My love for music is inspired by my father's devotion to it. I remember writing a poem about the ocean at four years old that my teacher was convinced I plagiarized. Apparently it was too sophisticated for a four-year-old (and a Black four-year-old at that). I remember my father, who used to play songs from the titans of jazz—John Coltrane, Sonny Rollins, Miles Davis—on our way to grab a slice of pizza after my karate classes, giving my teacher the read of a lifetime over the phone about that poem. Those pizza runs—listening to my father over the swell of music as he explained the depths of jazz's innovation and spoke to how this music impacted art and global culture as well as the happiness these songs brought him as a kid in Ghana—are part of the reason you're holding this book today.

My love for film and visual art is inspired by the moments my mother and I shared watching movies and cartoons together. My habit of watching and re-watching the same movie or show over and over again comes from our many hours of watching classic Disney shorts like *An Officer and a Duck* or the incomparable performances embedded in *The Godfather*. With each viewing, we found something new to laugh or marvel at—my mother showed me the infinite nature of artistic expression and interpretation.

Both my parents showed me the power of language as art. As an only child, I had plenty of time to absorb my parents' influences in our small townhouse outside of Washington, DC. My father's command of the English language is an art in and of itself. He speaks with no words wasted and can express himself with seemingly endless erudition on any topic. His way with words and his command of a room often landed him in the role of MC at various functions in the Ghanaian community. I, in psychological osmosis, soaked it all in. My mother speaks in a slightly more casual but no less masterful way. To hear her sing-song cadence is to be hypnotized in the best way; she speaks purely, compassionately, and honestly, with an underpinning of modest regality. To listen to my parents speak and to read their words, to have been immersed in them all my life, is a gift I cannot fully grasp.

When I was about seven, my mother became a Buddhist in the Sokka Gakkai/Nichiren tradition. On Sundays and some weekday nights, she brought me to the temple to light incense, chant, and pray. The golden sculptures, intricate calligraphies, and the flowing robes of the priests made an impact on me that I wouldn't fully realize until later. Over time, I began to absorb the foundations of Buddhism: that it is human to struggle and to suffer, and that there is a path to freedom from suffering. The Buddha was not a god, but a person like you and me who just happened to set out to solve the riddle of the human condition. His teachings: compassion and wisdom, are tools each of us can take up in approaching the riddle ourselves.

As a teenager, one seminal event transformed my life: discovering hip-hop. Hip-hop became my best friend, my older sibling, my teacher, and my therapist. Eventually I decided to make it my life. Hip-hop (and

Buddhism) freed me from the feelings of isolation and nihilism I experienced as I grew and gave my heart and mind a voice.

In college, my then-girlfriend now-wife and I discovered we were expecting our first child. I followed my intuition and immersed myself in the *Dharma*—the teachings of the Buddha—to prepare for fatherhood and the life journey to come. Perhaps the Buddhist wisdom tradition could help me cultivate the stability, kindness, and wisdom I would need to be a supportive and loving parent, I thought. The influence of those early years in the temple with my mother, coupled with an almost cosmic push toward the Dharma on behalf of this child, strengthened my spiritual conviction. The greatest gift I could offer my child, I thought, would be the Buddha's teachings of love and liberation. I recognized that this would involve facing and moving through my own suffering. "If we don't transform our pain, we'll transmit it," as priest and writer Richard Rohr says.

A chance encounter on the bus a few years later began my journey as a teacher. One day, I happened to sit across from a gentleman reading a Buddhist magazine. We struck up a conversation, and it turned out that he not only lived across the street from me, but was a Buddhist teacher specializing in teaching families the basic principles of the Dharma in fun, accessible ways. Carl Skooglund and I became friends, and my family became part of the *sangha*, or community, he had cultivated. One day, Carl suggested I join him as a guest teacher. I really enjoyed finding silly ways to share concepts like compassion and overcoming anger with the kids, and they seemed to find me entertaining, if nothing else. Carl began inviting me to guest teach more and more, until one day he announced his retirement and left guidance of the sangha and its classes to me and my dear friend Jennifer Jordan.

As society began to realize the science-backed value of mindfulness and meditation, I received more and more offers to teach. I often think of my teaching career as a series of happy accidents—I had many ambitions and intentions, but teaching was never one of them. In fact, I'm still a bit uncomfortable with the "teacher" title. When I think of my own teachers and inspirations—my parents and parents-in-law, my wife and children, my root teacher Bhante Buddharakkhita and masters like Osho Zenju Earthlyn Manuel,

Thích Nhất Hạnh, Ajahn Mun, Ajahn Chah, Ayya Anandabodhi, Bhante Gunaratana, His Holiness the Dalai Lama, Alice Coltrane, John Coltrane, Alice Walker, The RZA, Nas, Erykah Badu, H.E. Jetsunma Akhon Lhamo, Ven. Pannavatti, Tara Brach, Kōshō Uchiyama, and Suzuki Roshi—the list goes on—it's clear to me that, in the light of these incredible humans, I can hardly call myself a teacher.

I see myself as an encourager, someone on the ground level willing to share their experiences with difficulty, struggle, and relief. Mostly I want to encourage people to be kind to themselves, not to give up on themselves, and to keep returning to the path when they stumble. I hope to normalize the struggles we all face as humans and encourage people not to harm themselves or others—I know the pain of these harms well. If it is easier or more helpful to think of me as a teacher, please know I hold the title lightly *and* with deep reverence.

In the early years of my hip-hop journey, I wanted to be a full-time rapper. I didn't see how the worlds of hip-hop and Dharma could ever mix. In fact, I did everything I could to keep them separate, fearing I would lose my "edge" as a rapper if people knew I taught meditation and be perceived as "too edgy" if I allowed my rapper persona to coexist with my teaching role. Furthering this deluded approach, I also tried to keep my personal life and my struggles hidden, both as a rapper and teacher. Although I was suffering deeply with issues around mental health, substance abuse, personal identity, surviving sexual assault, and more, I rarely spoke about these challenges in my music or from the teacher's seat, fearing I would lose my respective audiences if I told the truth about how deeply in pain I was. Resonating with hip-hop as a listener felt far safer than expressing my truth as an artist.

Looking back, even though I know this was a misguided approach, I have compassion for my younger self, the artist and teacher afraid to share his struggles with the world. Over time, I've found the best way to connect with people is to simply be myself, whether in a song or on a retreat. In the role of a teacher, I have found it powerful to normalize our collective experience of suffering—no one is immune from the Buddha's first noble truth that suffering exists. As a hip-hop artist, it became important for me to drop the façades of bravado, materialism, and presumed mental health in my lyrics and to fully express the ups and downs of being human: my joys, failures, insights, and anxieties. As I became more comfortable sharing what was true in my experience, both from the teacher's seat and from behind the microphone, some core themes began to emerge: self-compassion, healing, and the wisdom of interbeing (everything is connected). These topics have become the foundation of all my work.

Though I am not an exemplary one, I am grateful to be a Buddhist practitioner. As a rapper, I'm passionate about sharing from the heart—which often includes how the Buddha's teachings have impacted my life—in a (hopefully) accessible way. I owe my parents a debt of gratitude I can never repay for setting me on the path of Dharmic artistry.

This book is a collection of lyrics from three albums—*In This Moment*, *AMIDA*, and *Komorebi* (a Japanese word that means "sunlight leaking through the trees"). Some lyrics are followed by breakdowns to highlight themes, backstories, Dharma teachings, and insights, while others are left to speak for themselves without further explanation. Everything in these pages can be read as poetry. You can listen to the songs while reading to deepen the experience of both the book and the music. Feel free to flip to any verse at any time, or to read front to back. Back to front will work, too. Return to a particular verse, line, breakdown, or story as many times as it speaks to you. Take your time. Feel free—this book is yours.

These days, I'm happy to say I am more in touch with a sense of peace within myself, a peace which was once so elusive. It's been hard, and in many cases I made it harder than it needed to be (for myself and others), but I can feel a more peaceful heart emerging now, like the sunlight leaking through the trees: *komorebi*. It doesn't mean life is easy, just that I can stay a bit more centered as I roll with its punches. Healing remains a process. I share my life through art and anecdotes with the hope that you come away with the following messages tattooed on your heart: be kind to yourself, don't give up on yourself, continue to pursue your greatest aspirations, keep rising no matter how many times you fall down, and remember—"every new breath is a chance, every new step is a dance."

In short: you are enough.

*What we experience in meditation*
*is of a realm beyond the reach*
*of language.*

*So how to express the ineffable?*
*Perhaps through experience itself.*

—EDWARD BURGER

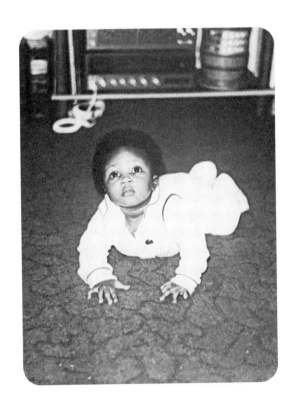

# The Hun- dreds

wrote a hundred rhymes
like a hundred times
blew a hundred lines
like a hundred times
listen for the sniff
I ain't hard to find
walking in the dark
I was colorblind

I lived a hundred lives
like a hundred times
for every pot of gold
I found a way to undermine
almost lost my wife
like a hundred times
what do you see in me?
she told me love is blind
hundred hours of meditation
like a hundred times
I must've cried at least a hundred
thousand times
attempted suicide a couple times
saved by the power
when understanding and love

combine
all the shit I did to numb my mind
so many bottles
vampires said my blood was wine
or rather Tito's
shout out to my amigos
who tuck the nine
for coming in the clutch
like a hundred times
call my therapist
discussion time
turns out the pain that I was holding
really wasn't mine
still I had to heal from it

for the hundredth time
underlying fears turn to thoughts
and become the mind
from Noah's ark to Napoleon Bonaparte
I was blown apart
a hero in disguise
like I am Joan of Arc
I know the feeling
when it's cold and dark
spiritual surgery
preferred me with an open heart

ooooooooo...
I've tried a hundred times
ooooooooo...
I've cried a hundred times
ooooooooo...
I've died a hundred times

I walk quietly to the altar in my bedroom. I light incense, place it on the altar, and bow. Then I sit cross-legged on my meditation cushion, facing the wall as is customary in Soto Zen. The wall represents my mind, a symbol of the veil I'm working to see through, the karma I'm practicing to transcend. I've faced this inner wall hundreds of times, cried at this wall, tried my best to scale it, only to fall again and again. Hundreds and hundreds of times.

Beyond the physical wall I'm facing, today the wall in my mind holds up hundreds of photos and moving pictures, showing me all the unskillful ways I have spent my life, all the ways I've suffered, all the ways I've tried to run from my suffering, all the ways I've tried to heal and make

sense of my life. I feel the impact of spinning my wheels in these painful cycles again and again, of walking uphill and downhill in spirals that feel like closed circles. Part of my heart, part of my soul, part of my mind feels utterly exhausted from countless therapy sessions, moments of real and attempted self-harm, and dealing with the monster of OCD day in and day out. It's all taken its toll. In my exhaustion, in compassion for myself, I've had to make changes. As I sit in meditation, the wall I face today is a wall of changes.

Each change has been significant, challenging, humbling, sad, powerful, and liberating. These days I spend more time in temples than clubs, more time offering sound baths than sound bites. It's been years now since

I've been on the party-to-be-seen, afterparty scene. My entourage is my wife and children, along with my fellow practitioners and the friends whom I've called family since day one. My favorite drinks are water, oat milk lattes, and hibiscus tea. I broke up with my dealer long ago.

After meditating, I reach out for more help. A new therapist finally gives me an actual diagnosis and eventually suggests medicine to help ease my OCD symptoms. I feel a mix of relief and humiliation at being a practitioner, a teacher, and an artist who needs so much help, but I think of what I would say to a best friend or a loved one in the same situation and know I would completely support them taking care of themselves however they could. Knowing this reduces my humiliation a bit, and I can allow myself to be humbled by being human. The medication I take is an expression of compassion for myself. I refer to it as "the Medicine Buddha."

One of the most significant changes has been how I approach meditation. Although I initially trained to keep my attention in one place—either on my breathing, physical sensations, or sounds—I have found that practicing with a sense of openness, of open awareness, feels much healthier. These days, I simply sit and watch things change. It's been liberating to find an approach to meditation that allows me to practice without enduring unnecessary cycles of pain, anxiety, and shame. When I sit, I leave the door open for meditation to happen. I don't force or expect anything. I don't try to achieve anything. If intrusive thoughts arise, I meet them with love or just let them pass without engaging. If I'm really struggling, I might mentally whisper the name *Avalokiteshvara* to activate the energy of compassion in my mind and embrace whatever pain is there with loving awareness. Mostly, though, I just sit and watch things change or, as Shunryu Suzuki Roshi puts it, "... sit and observe the universal activity, that is all."

Facing this wall of changes, I feel into the impermanence of the sounds from the street outside that come and go, the hum of engines that fill the air with vibrations and quickly drift into silence. A crow's call breaks the silence—the ancestral voice of my grandmother, reassuring me. I remain open. I return to the wall. I watch things change. Thoughts arise, some pleasant, some painful, some neutral. They drift through the sky of my mind like drops of indigo ink in a large body

# I don't force or
## expect anything.

# I don't try to
## achieve anything.

of clear water. The water perpetually refreshes itself; the ink fades into vastness. I return to the wall. I watch things change.

My music has become my practice. I've written hundreds of songs. Hundreds that may never be heard by anyone but me—they reflect times in my life I don't want to perpetuate or relive. Music that expresses my spiritual path and celebrates how the Dharma guides my relationship with life is the music my heart most deeply wants to make. Facing the wall of changes, I see the past, my suffering, and my many attempts to reconcile and heal my life.

Within this wall is a song that wants to be written. My duty is to watch the wall in silence, to let the song write itself. For the first time in my life, I feel mentally healthy. Hundreds of thousands of hours, tens of thousands of days to get here. No time wasted.

*I know the feeling when it's cold and dark*
*spiritual surgery preferred me with an open heart.*

●

# Being Enough

being enough is like being in love
walking with my feet in the dust
while I'm reaching above
when they feel the healing of love
what do demons become
I'm believing in love
where my peoples is from
I think that
being enough is like being in love

when I'm feeling as free as a dove
is my freedom enough?
could it be that believing in love
is the meaning of love
where my peoples is from
all that we could become
praying with my
knees in the dust
'til my knees full of blood
praying I can expand it broadcast it
and deepen my love
I've retreated from love
hit the streets with my thugs
finding Jesus in love
Buddha's breathing is love
zazen

sitting still in the evening is love
the flowing breeze
blowing steam off the tea in my cup
what we speaking on cuz?
what we need to discuss?
I know grieving is tough
I been dreaming of love
I feel like
being enough is like being in love
legacies of what
colonial Europeans corrupt
trauma that became
the music fashion and people we love
trauma that became
the code of honor where secrets are dug

I feel like
being enough is like being in love
I know that feeling
when you question your reason for love
I know the feeling when you finally
meeting the plug
and now you're helping all your people
but feeling corrupt
you're insulated from 'em
when all they needed was love
so all the sweating and the tears
didn't equal the blood
I've retreated from love
been depleted from drugs

finding Jesus in love
Buddha's breathing is love
the moon reflected off the water
this evening is love
Ayanna I will love you
until there's seas on the sun
my children I will love you
until infinity's done
the chances I survived my youth
was a million to one
I feel like
being enough is like being in love
poetry that I breathe in my lungs
becomes speaking in tongues
completed on drums
repeat it you'll see it
gets deeper for seasons to come
from evening to sun
from Neo to one
what we have accomplished
with love and knowledge
is really not frequently done
being enough
freedom in love
knowing there isn't any difference
between me and love
no separation in between
you and me is enough
to believe in this love
to be free in this love
maybe enlightenment's as
simple as being enough

# Om Mani Padme Hum

# CHAPTER THREE

**Thầy (Thích Nhất Hạnh):**
if you are motivated by a desire
to transform yourself
and to help your people
your community to transform
to bring joy and hope into their lives
then you have the best kind of volition
and that gives you an infinite source of energy
you become very alive, very dynamic in your daily life

om mani padme hum

# (Tribute)

Thầy:

mindfulness helps us to be established in the here and now
and that is the basic condition for us to touch life
to touch the kingdom of God
to touch the pure land of the Buddha

**Born I:**

life is still a mystery
futuristic history
couldn't see the present
and I used to let it get to me
healing transformation
needed amputation
from the things I was afraid of
for my inner activation
I was watching Aristotle
philosophies I borrow
yesterday is not tomorrow
so today is what I follow
gifted by the present
I'm lifted by the presence
of my great grandmother
who predicted my ascendence
so why I feel so low though
really I don't know though
maybe it's the coco

or the fear of living slo-mo
or maybe it's the vocals
of the teachings I ignored so
now I feel it in my spirit
manifested in my torso
I admit I'm blinded
women gold and diamonds
all my insecurities
expressed through my desires
take it for the love of it
hate myself because it
still I sit in meditation
waiting for the mothership
what have I discovered
through my blood
and through my struggles
maybe wisdom is the belt
and then compassion is the buckle
recognize the emptiness
combined with inner friendliness
if I ever forget it
I just pray that I remember this

**Thầy:**
you know the children have the capacity
of being in the here and the now
more than adults
they don't think too much about the future
they don't make a lot of projects like we do
and they are not caught in the past, by the past
so learning to be more like children
is a good practice

**Born I:**
the answer is the question
the question is the answer
love and understanding
represented by the mantra

in this world of murder and fear and hate
hard to figure out what is real and fake
all my travels across the interstate
took me deeper into that inner place
beginner's mind is silence
ignorance is violence
anxiety is terrible
and mine is so unbearable
that if I ever overcome it
it'll be a miracle
I know I'm here to witness who I am
but through the mirrors view
every day is heaven
every day is hell
every day I fall apart
every day I prevail
rising and the falling
like the night into the morning
I've been fighting all along
to be a light inside the storm but
maybe I should let it go
scan the body head to toe
and hold myself with kindness
when self-hatred is susceptible
understand the moment
is another passing episode

and if it gets too difficult
I just take a breath and go


om mani padme hum


**Thầy:**
it's like a wave
on the surface of the ocean
she may be very fearful
because she gets caught in notions like
beginning, ending
going up, going down
more or less beautiful
than the other waves
but if the wave
is aware
that she is water
and then she loses all this kind of fear
going up she is joyful
going down she is joyful
because she knows that she is water
she is not only a wave
she is also water

isn't exactly a mainstream concept. Making this music, I find myself afraid, vulnerable, naked. As a rapper, I want my songs to speak for themselves. This book asks me to speak to the deeper meanings, experiences, pathologies, aspirations, failings, and ambitions of the real, everyday life behind the songs. As a Black man, a teacher, a parent, a husband, and a child, I feel afraid and uneasy about sharing the various hearts within my heart. I struggled with writing this particular chapter all day, until I just surrendered and asked the book: What do you want me to write about? This is me, getting out of the way and letting the book write itself.

My new friend, filmmaker Edward Burger, wrote an article about the "Buddhist contemplative gaze"—a way of seeing and being in the world that reflects the connection between the inner and outer realities of our moment-to-moment existence. As a filmmaker and Buddhist, Edward feels called to bring this contemplative gaze into every area of his life, including his life as an artist. His films are an extension, reflection, and expression of engaging with reality on a deep, contemplative level. As a rapper, writer, and Buddhist meditator, I feel very connected to this philosophy in which the in-look meets the outlook of the Buddhist contemplative gaze. Erasing the distinction between my spiritual practice and my art, allowing the two to become one, is what this book is really about, what my life is about: art as practice. Practice as art. Life as practice. Practice as life. Writing this book, gazing upon and sharing

# We can find our stories

# in the stories of others

from the heart, is both terrifying and healing. It is the only way.

I once read a comment online: "Shared experience is the destruction of shame." I've taken these words to heart. Many of us suffer in silence and shame needlessly. Human beings are more alike than we might believe, and when we share our individual truths with honesty and vulnerability, we give others permission to do the same. We can find our stories in the stories of others and begin to realize our unique sufferings are not so unique after all. Sharing my art from the heart is a part of my own healing process, but it is also an offering—may it give you some inspiration to be free from shame and feelings of separation from your fellow humans, or at least from *this* fellow human.

To write today, I had to surrender. I had to ask what wanted to be said and then step away, listen, connect with other work, feel the frustration of writer's block, drive in a thunderstorm to help my father move a patio umbrella, wash the dishes, feel down, feed my children, meditate, and finally, express what wanted to be expressed. It's a reminder that this book is also my practice. There is no separation.

The mantra *om mani padme hum* is about the inseparability of wisdom and compassion as the ingredients for awakening: the wisdom that everything in existence is intertwined and the compassion that expresses this understanding as kindness. Life is art. Art is practice. Practice is life. In these lyrics, in this book, I am unarmed and unarmored. It's scary. It's the only way. This book is a way of liberating myself from these stories, so many of which are stories of deep suffering. Coming into writing this chapter, I found myself exhausted, no longer wanting to relive these stories. The art has been made. This is a moment of liberation. Om mani padme hum.

# Equi-
# nox

when I'm just sitting and seeing
swim in the river of being
thirsty for knowledge but when I dissolve
it's beyond just the literal meaning
after nirvana the laundry
after enlightenment dishes
all that I know is
there's only this moment
and never a higher position
what could inspire my vision?

open my eyes and I listen
total surprise
when I'm going inside
and I know what I find
is defying description
I'm never dying a victim
raising a child with my wisdom
dream of the shore
but the feeling is raw
when I look at the miles in the distance

answering calls from the prison line
told him to chill and just give it time
still when you can't see your children
even in the summer
it's cold as the wintertime
some of my people move packages
beef and then speak to the mattresses
if you could see all my damages
doubt you could ever believe how I managed it

kneeling and noticing breaths
I feel the wind
move in and out of my chest
silence is loudest
when I think about it
I'm emptying out until nothing is left
moments can never be broken
sit and reflect on a quote
that can never be spoken
let it be known I'm content to be sewn
as the fabric upon which the effigy's woven
freedom is all that we are
see in myself everything
that I see in the stars
sometimes I weep and I sob
loving myself is the same as believing in God
I try to let it all go
stay in the present within the perpetual flow
where do we go when it's done
into the sun?
only the heavens can know
burning the slowest of candles
watching the butterfly go
when I open my hand up
this is a koan
when stillness can flow on
the freedom of knowing
I don't know the answer
hell is behind us
best we can do is to let it remind us
hell is behind us
presence and kindness
ended my blindness

# In This Moment

# CHAPTER FIVE

Look at yourself in this moment
ask yourself how do you feel
all that you know is the moment
that's the only thing that's real
Look at yourself in this moment
ask yourself how do you feel
all that you have is this moment
That's the only thing that's real

Moments they come and these moments they go
if we come back again it's the infinite flow
but until then we're still in this moment forever
the past is forgotten
the future is never
the present is all that we know and can measure
joy and the pain and the pain and the pleasure
making it better or making it worse
if it's the second then make it reverse
until the day that I'm laid in a hearse
I'm a just be out here making it work
I fell in love with cocaine it's a flirt
search for the feeling escaping the hurt
mix it with Tito's
don't mix it with needles
I'm wet like a fish and I'm high like an eagle
becoming the villain supplying my ego
one moment a hero the next one I'm evil
I don't know who I am half of the time
let it all go if I black out it's fine
I'm sick of dealing with life it's a chore
really don't want to feel nothing no more
do it from sundown to sundown again
bracing myself for the comedown again
hating myself in the comedown again
wait for the party to come round again
I know my teacher would be disappointed
all of the training he gave me was pointless
but even though right now I feel like I'm worthless
Imma just look at my mind and observe it

Ask yourself how do you feel
All that you know is this moment
that's the only thing that's real
Look at yourself in this moment
ask yourself how do you feel
all that you know is this moment
that's the only thing that's real

I try to focus excitement
sit in the lotus alignment
the truth is that I want to know what's inside
and the Buddha said you'll never know till you try it
so I sit in silence and steady my breathing
and try to see something I've never believed in
I want to know every
part of my soul
part of my soul
how it develops and how it unfolds
all these emotions lock me in a prison
soon as I notice they're gone in an instant
knock knock who's there when the door swings
Robin Hood with an arrow and a bow with strings
look for the light at the end of the tunnel
all of the ways I defended my struggle
I am the child
I am the parent
I am illusion
I am awareness
I am the pain that I didn't take care of
that turned into all of the things that I'm scared of
what do I notice is none of it lasts

same as the lightning and thunder that crash
all of the thoughts and the feelings and fears
stay for a moment and then disappear
everything in me is naturally free
all that's required is I let it be
I am the sun
I am the storm
they called me Infinite when I was Born
I am enough
is the mantra repeated
for all of the love and compassion that's needed
and yes I might fall again but
Then I'll rise again
sitting cross-legged
and closing my eyes again
and closing my eyes again
and closing my eyes again

Look at yourself in this moment
Ask yourself how do you feel
All that you have is this moment
That's the only thing that's real
Look at yourself in this moment
Ask yourself how do you feel
All that you know is this moment
That's the only thing that's real

**I'm jolted out** of sleep. I shudder. Tears well up in my eyes as I attempt to calm my breathing. Another nightmare. This time, I was desperately searching for a friend I couldn't find. The horror of the dream was my already knowing why I couldn't find him, yet continuing to search in desperation anyway. It was torture. Awake, I remind myself it was only a dream. I am right here, right now, in this moment.

I wrote "In This Moment" during a battle with deep depression. The COVID-19 pandemic had just shut down all travel, and my touring plans were abruptly canceled. Before the shutdown, I had been moving at a very fast pace, always traveling, recording, performing, teaching, or parenting. At home, tending to the needs of our four children left my wife and I little room for downtime. Amid all this activity, I'd avoided the depths of grief thrust upon me the previous summer when my manager and dear friend Tom Dern had died suddenly at the age of twenty-nine. I considered Tom more than a friend or manager. He was my brother. Unsure of how to process the sadness and fear I felt after his passing, I buried myself in my work and tried to complete all the goals he and I had set as a way of honoring his memory and our vision.

Tom saw the potential for me to put my skills as a rapper to use outside of hip-hop by pivoting to rapping over electronic music (EDM). It was a bold gamble, and it paid off. In a short time, I had become a sought-after vocalist in various subgenres of EDM, working with some of the biggest names in the industry and performing at festivals like EDC Vegas in front of crowds of over 30,000 people. Together, Tom and I had done something unprecedented. Before he died, we had made plans to release a hip-hop/EDM hybrid album that would be the culmination of our shared vision.

In the summer of 2018, I recorded the album *Gold Chains and Meditation* (ultimately never released) and sent it to record labels for consideration. It was that August, while I taught a meditation retreat and talked plans with Tom during my downtime, that he called and spoke of terrible back pain. Tom went to the ER, where it turned out he needed surgery. We spoke after his emergency operation; he had refused opioids for fear of their addictive capacity and was in intense agony as a result. The next day, Tom was dead. "Complications from the operation," they said.

My little brother was gone. My world fell apart.

In the following months, I tried to put things back together. I pressed on—I shopped the new album, released singles, and recorded new music. I tried to accomplish what Tom and I had set out to do. In the process, I stopped caring if I was on the right creative path or if I even enjoyed what I was doing. I filled the hollowness inside with more and more work, justified by the idea of finishing Tom's mission and providing for my family. I numbed myself with alcohol, work, and false stoicism. For a while, it seemed like everything was taking shape, moving forward.

Then the world stopped.

During the pandemic lockdowns, I could no longer run from myself— though not for lack of trying. First, I tried to escape through self-

medicating with alcohol and drugs, but this only made things worse. Next, I tried to disappear internally through long periods of daily sitting meditation practice. The irony of this approach, though, is that meditation is about opening to whatever arises, whatever is there—it's about stopping, about not trying to escape. The more I sat with myself, the less I could ignore the deep pain, deep sadness, and deep shame churning within me. I had lost myself, I realized. In the process of trying to become a successful artist and a provider for my family, in the process of *not processing* Tom's death—deeper still, in not processing the traumas I had experienced throughout my life and in trying to hide from my own shadow—I had become, I now felt, a walking death. Internally and externally, I was slowly killing myself.

Day in and day out, I sat in meditation, crushed under the heaviness of these feelings. One day, my wife, Ayanna found me in our bedroom, sobbing. "I'm falling apart," I told her, "I don't know what to do." The next day, she searched the internet for a therapist and found Dr. Josue, a Black man originally from Haiti, who connected with me in a kind and empathetic way. He told me frankly, "You're telling everyone to be kind to themselves, but you're not taking your own advice." Over the next six months, he put me through what I like to call a "self-compassion bootcamp."

Every morning after meditation, I wrote myself a letter acknowledging my suffering and offering myself the kind words and encouragement of a friend. I would write things like, "Ofosu, I know you miss Tom and that you're scared, I'm sorry things are so hard right now. I believe in you," or, "Dear Ofosu, I am sorry for the pain you experienced as a child, it wasn't your fault." I listened to affirmations of self-love and self-acceptance by Louise Hay. I talked to my parents about my feelings and about my life, told them things they didn't know I had gone through—sexual assault as a child, drug use, and more. I talked

# I talked with my wife, I cried often, and she listened, holding my pain like the sky holds clouds.

with my wife, I cried often, and she listened, holding my pain like the sky holds clouds. Most importantly, I talked to myself. I expressed my sadness, fears, and self-loathing and responded with words of love, encouragement, and forgiveness. I also began to read *Reconciliation: Healing the Inner Child* by Thích Nhất Hạnh. This profound work and the practical skills for healing past traumas Nhất Hạnh offers helped guide my steps on the path of healing.

Meanwhile, the pandemic raged. Death continued to hover over our lives. My wife's aunt Eileen (Aunt Lee), who was very dear to us all, died of COVID-19 complications. My own mortality became glaringly apparent. I started to wonder, *If I were to die today, what would I leave behind for my children?* Not materially, per se, but spiritually, artistically. *How would they know what I truly was about, in my heart? How would they know what I wanted them to know and be able to use my life as a guide for their own?* As I reflected on death, I realized I wanted to share my two life paths—hip-hop and Dharma—as one expression. This would be my offering to my children, to my friend's memory, to the world.

This approach harkened back to my early days as an artist, when I was a member of the Dharma-inspired rap group Shambhala alongside my brother Agua, and we created the underground album *The Lotus Of....* When I went solo, I walked away from this blended vision. Now it was time to return, but in a new way, reborn. I reached out to my friend Lorenzo Best, aka Linz Prag—an extremely talented music producer—and asked him to send me a beat that felt like a "spiritual trap." He sent me a track with a deep, hypnotic, living bassline punctuated with stuttering hi-hats. This bass-heavy python of a track, adorned with a flute melody that sounded like a story being told from both the past and the future while finding resolution in the present, slithered like the legendary *nagas*, the dragon-like beings who protect the Buddha's teachings. The beat inspired and intimidated me. Not knowing what to write at first, I meditated to the beat. Slowly, the words arose in me: "Look at yourself in this moment, ask yourself how do you feel, all that you know is this moment, that's the only thing that's real."

Writing "In This Moment" was a sad, beautiful, life-changing experience. In all my years of writing, I had never written anything quite as raw, genuine, and honest as this song. When it was done, it felt like the song I had been waiting to write for my entire life. Today, I still consider "In This Moment" one of my most important songs.

The first verse is a story of contrast. It begins with me sharing what I know, at least academically, about the Dharma, teachings on the present moment, and karma. I'm struck by how much sadness and despair the lyrics convey. Clearly, I was suffering deeply. I didn't care if I lived or died. Even though I had knowledge of the path of liberation, even though I had teachers, parents, therapists, and family who cared for me and pointed out the way, my heart was aching, my actions were still unskillful, I was hurting. But something transformative happens at the end of the first verse: even in

# In all my years of writing, I had never written anything quite as raw, genuine, and honest as this song.

the middle of my despair, the practice of meditation—looking deeply into my own mind, heart, and life—didn't abandon me.

The chorus to "In This Moment" is a reminder to myself that only in the present moment can life truly be experienced. From the Buddha to Zenju Earthlyn Manuel to Thích Nhất Hạnh and my root teacher Bhante Buddharakkhita, all my Dharma teachers have taught that life can only be lived in the present moment. The past is a memory, and the future is a fabrication. Only in the present moment can we make sense of the past and affect the future. The three times—past, present, and future— exist only in the now.

Where the first verse paints a picture of despair with a glimmer of hope, the second verse reveals what happens when I look at myself with eyes of compassion. Instead of judging myself and feeling worthless, I sit with myself and begin trying to understand my suffering, both in my heart and mind, and this creates a shift. Even when I felt I was completely falling apart, I turned my attention inward. By coming home to myself in meditation, I experienced the impermanence of my emotional turmoil. Though it felt never-ending, when I made space to be with my

experience, no pain was constant; emotions—positive, negative, and neutral—revealed themselves as thoroughly temporary. By bringing kind attention to the thoughts and emotions as they arose within me, the thoughts and emotions liberated themselves.

The more I looked underneath the waves of thoughts and emotions, the more understanding emerged: my suffering wasn't only mine alone, but a part of the suffering of all beings. It was connected to my childhood, to my parents, to their childhood and their parents, to the whole story of humanity.

*I am the child*
*I am the parent*
*I am illusion*
*I am awareness*
*I am the pain that I didn't take care of*
*that turned into all of the things that*
*I'm scared of*

When I wrote those lines, two things happened: first, I felt proud of myself artistically for writing something that really encapsulated how I felt. I had written something unlike anything I had written before. This inspired me to resolve that instead of trying to present myself as a rapper who had it all figured out, sending mixed messages by writing "positive lyrics" that dabbled in the tropes of materialism and hypersexuality, my music from now on would be about my practice, the liberative Buddhist Dharma, and my journey to heal and overcome suffering.

I needed to go further. Just because I had understood my suffering was connected to trauma I hadn't taken care of didn't mean that was the end of it. If suffering itself is impermanent, it doesn't have to be the end of my story. Buddhism centers four insights the Buddha had after awakening and freeing himself from suffering, known as the Four Noble Truths: suffering exists, suffering has causes, suffering can come to an end, and there is a path to this freedom. The Third Noble Truth, that suffering can come to an end, birthed a deeper understanding in me as I looked at my situation through the eyes of meditation.

Allowing thoughts, emotions, sensations, and mental formations to simply arise, abide for a little bit, and then fade away on their own showed me through embodied experience that the nature of everything is freedom. From a summer breeze to my own heartbeat, everything in life arises and changes according to causes and conditions. Nothing remains the same, nothing lasts forever. There is

freedom in this ever-changing nature of life. Life is freedom itself. I'm not stuck in place, I'm free to change, I'll always change, put forth different causes and conditions, heal, and transform.

The end of the song is an offering of grace and compassion to myself. It reminds me I am enough and invites anyone listening, reading, or singing along to remember that they are, too. While it's entirely possible for me, for us, to stumble and fall, I know unequivocally that by going inward, we can get back up, come back to the path, and keep going.

*I am enough*
*is the mantra repeated*
*for all of the love and compassion*
*that's needed*
*and yes I might fall again but*
*then I'll rise again*
*sitting cross-legged*
*and closing my eyes again*

# Silent Illumina- tion

breath is love and love is all
softer than the breeze
that turns the summer into fall
form is emptiness and emptiness is form
I'm breathing in a quiet place
where memories are born

sittin' hours long in poses
plus the power of enforcers
turned me from an ogre
to a flower garden stroller
komorebi photographer
holding heavy binoculars
each falling leaf
is a slow and steady provocateur
perpetual evaporation
no matter how you move
the decimals and calculations
the mystery reinvents
pray I'm a great grandfather
when my breathing relents
finally I want to live
romanticizing death is
just the luxury of kids
Amitabha Avalokiteshvara
my son and daughters
fathered by a foolish man
to prove destiny in nirvana
blessings can now befall us
devils can only stall us
we adopt the mind of Joseph
when heaven's messengers call us
seven steps in the garden
or sending flesh to piranhas
or a bodhisattva
holding a treasure chest
for the farmers

take a breath
take a breath

Buddha Dharma and Sangha
Dharma Sangha and Buddha
me and Ayanna like
Mogallana and Sariputra
a liturgical reference
if ever you read the suttas
Allen Iverson provides
if you ever need a computer
young Bruce Wayne watching Zorro
Born I sipping Suntory
mixed with Sapporo
the relevance is Dali
Salvatore Mundi
lamas is in the lobby
promises often haunt me
my common sense was Atari
the levels built with my Ahkis
was my eventual sorrys
but why apologize for livin'?
my teacher told me
only I could compromise my sittin'
thank you God for this moment
I know it could be worse
with even harder components
I invited Ka's spirit to enter me
to be a conduit
an expression of legacy
time keeps turning

the mind keeps yearning
fire sermon says that everything
my eyes see burnin'
returning to the source
between the rhythm of my thoughts
even in the deepest silence
know the rhythm isn't lost
little did I know
what losing innocence would cost
all the obstacles
that I would come to witness
through the course

take a breath
take a breath

meditation at the tree of resilience
the hollow trunk reveals the burns
I can feel in my feelings
hard to extinguish all the fires
I redeem while I'm healing
hard to distinguish from the visions
that I see when I'm kneeling
I'm being enough as I spy the sublime
walking the mountains
dancing with the sunlight through the pines
time after time brokenhearted the life of my dime
spiraling chimes punctuated my life full of crimes
I'm being enough as a learn and unfold
the words I compose
fly away as a murder of crows

soon as the moment good and evil
converge in my soul,
a new awakening begins to emerge and unfold
this is shikantaza
sit and breathe
and leave the peace to Mama
some repeat the horror
some go deep
and then complete the saga

breath

take a breath

# Koan

looking deep into the riverbed
I wrote this song at the river's edge
asked it a question then I closed my eyes
and I listened and here's what the river said
everything's a part of something else
everything depends on something else
if there's no causes and there's no conditions
then nothing can give rise unto itself

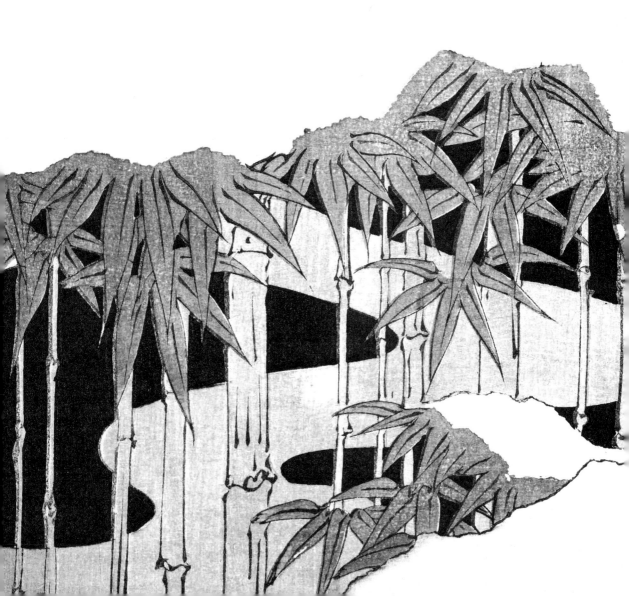

dependent origination
I try to see with investigation
no matter how clear it is I still have fear of it
I can't explain all my hesitation
like watching the leaves fall in autumn
big Ernest I couldn't believe when they shot him
or how they left him to bleed when they dropped him
crying, weeping, wheezing, coughing
I'm on a riverbank he's in a coffin
repeating the cycle I'll see you in autumn
you and I watching the leaves fall again
no matter your form you will still be my friend
thinking deep
thinking deep
thinking deep
I was awake but I'm still asleep
deep in the forest while on retreat
understanding all my suffering begins with me
meditation when my eyes are closed
somehow still dressed in the flyest clothes
10,000 recitations of the Mantra to Padmasambhava
my mind is blown

who the Zen student and who the master?
which one of us gets to Buddha faster?
this is a koan more like one to grow on
don't think I could ever give you the answer

sometimes I feel out of place
body's on earth but my mind is in space
dream of the past I'm rewinding the dates

but I'm still in the present applying for grace
scared of the ripple effects
of the purchases that keep my spirit in debt
and though I know that what I fear isn't death
but on my deathbed the appearance of stress
breathing in breathing out I used to need the crown
now I just dream about how I can even out
used to think I had to cast all my demons out
now I just give them love when they see me around
breathing in/breathing out
funny how badly we want to be free when bound
all of the screaming crowds
now when the speakers sound
*om mani padme hum* is the most frequent sound
contemplation at the water's edge
my teacher said give it your all instead
I tried to do the bare minimum
all it gave me was the turmoil I'm swimming in
now I'm more synchronized
open my blinking eyes
if there's no mud there's no lotus
I realize I'm looking deep inside
what do I see inside?
only compassion and wisdom can free my mind

who the Zen student and who the master?
which one of us gets to Buddha faster?
this is a koan more like one to grow on
don't think I could ever give you the answer

**At the edge of a river,** the riddle of life and death expresses itself to me, asking me to solve the unsolvable. I wrote "Koan" while co-teaching an autumn meditation retreat for the Insight Meditation Community of Washington in 2022. Sevenoaks Retreat Center in the Shenandoah mountains of Virginia, a beautiful open area of towering oaks, vibrant ginkgo trees, and lush forest surrounded by mountains, hosted the retreat. About a mile into the forest is a river where people sometimes enjoy tubing in the summer. When it's warm, it's not uncommon to see deer crossing shallow parts of the river or groundhogs scuttling about the banks. In the distance, you can hear cows from a nearby farm; if you look into the water itself, darting fish of various sizes become visible. When autumn comes, the river flows more

slowly, gently. One by one, leaves fall into the water from the trees above—an expression of the impermanence of all things.

About three days into intensive periods of sitting and walking meditation, I walked down to the river and sat at the edge during a break in the retreat. Looking into the water and watching the leaves fall, lyrics began to form in my mind as an expression of what was on my heart.

*looking deep into the riverbed*
*I wrote this song at the river's edge*
*asked it a question then I closed*
*my eyes*
*and I listened and here's what the*
*river said*

For centuries, Zen masters have used *koans*, a type of riddle, as tools to confound logical thinking and bring the student's mind face-to-face with the ineffable nature of reality beyond dualistic concepts. This shattering of the conceptual intellect can create the conditions for awakening. When I wrote this song, I had just returned from Plum Village monastery in France a few months earlier. Practicing Zen in the tradition of one of my dear teachers, the great Zen master Thích Nhất Hạnh (or Thầy, as he is known—an affectionate

Vietnamese term for "teacher"), I remembered a line from his book *Inside the Now*:

If what the Buddha taught about non-self is true, then who is the Zen master? Is the Zen master who is teaching you a self? Who are you? Who is the Zen master? The Buddha has made it very clear: there is no self. Who is the one reciting the Buddha's name? It is me. Yet I do not really know who I am— that is why I am searching for myself.

I had heard this line recited by my friend and teacher, the nun Sister True Dedication, while I was in Plum Village, and it struck me very deeply as a koan that at once brought a feeling of oneness with everything and everyone around me. In an instant, I felt there was no real difference between Thầy, the Zen master Thích Nhất Hạnh—or any teacher, for that matter—and myself, no difference between me and the trees and birds around me, no separation whatsoever. In that moment, I felt liberation. I felt awakened to a deeper understanding of reality.

As my habitual, dualistic mind came back online, full of self-doubt, I returned to feeling a deep chasm

of difference between myself and Thầy. My perspective had shifted, though—I had been given a glimpse of something. Deep questions remained: Who am I? Who is the Zen master? I kept this koan in my heart.

Sitting on the riverbank at Sevenoaks Retreat Center, I watched leaves dancing in the air on their way down to the water. Each leaf had a story, a journey nourished by earth, wind, water, and sun, containing all of these elements within it as it gave energy to its tree, oxygen to animals, shade to travelers, and food to insects before eventually falling into the river to become another elemental configuration. I thought of the Buddha's teaching on dependent origination: there is no inherent, permanent self in anything. All that we are, all that we see and experience, is a series of impermanent, interdependent, ever-changing relationships. We are literally intimately connected with everything, transforming into and out of everything, ceaselessly. Seeing, feeling, and considering all of this, I wrote the next lines as the river spoke to me in its suchness:

*everything's a part of something else*
*everything depends on something else*

As much as I understand conceptually that everything is connected and that everything changes, as much as I can see this as beautiful in leaves and rivers, the part of me that wants to hold on to my identity as Ofosu, the human, the father, the husband, the rapper, the teacher, hesitates at the edge of reality's true nature. Is there really no birth and no death? Is there really nothing to be afraid of?

When I think of death—my own and the death of the people I love—I feel afraid, and I feel sad. While at Plum Village, one of my dear friends lost her teenage son in a tragic accident. A few months earlier, my friend Ernest was shot to death at a party; his killer is still at large to this day. How do these tragedies line up with my understanding of dependent origination? Where are my friends now? Where is my friend's teenage child now? What will I be when I die? What will happen to my wife, children, and parents when they die? Where is Thầy? I looked into the river with my heart, I looked at the trees overhead, their branches blurred by my tears, and I continued to listen.

*like watching the leaves fall*
*in autumn*
*big Ernest I couldn't believe when*
*they shot him*

*or how they left him to bleed when*
*they dropped him*
*crying, weeping, wheezing, coughing*
*I'm on a riverbank he's in a coffin*
*repeating the cycle I'll see you*
*in autumn*
*you and I watching the leaves*
*fall again*
*no matter your form you will still be*
*my friend*

As a single leaf fell from the bough of a tree, the wind created ripples over the water and the river told me about freedom and continuation. I couldn't stop the flow of things as they are, no matter how perplexing or distressing they might be. Seeing things clearly, birth and death are just names we ascribe to the inevitable changes everything experiences. Birth and death are ideas, not reality itself. My feelings about birth and death are the result of my ideas about ideas, and they are also subject to change. My beloved friend Tom speaks to me through memories; he speaks to me any time I see the number 11:11 on the clock; he is there any time I achieve something special in my music career, any time I hear his voice in my mind—he is there. My friend Ernest is alive in my heart, and his energy travels through the universe not just as a matter of scientific fact, but through all the lives he touched while he was in the flesh-and-bone form we knew as "Ernest." My friend's child will continue to be a part of her life forever, no matter their form. Whenever I see the wind dancing through pine needles, I know Thầy is there.

The entire experience of sitting on the edge of the river, feeling into the nature of birth and death, the nature of reality, and trying to understand my place in it all was beyond words. Even though I've now written about what I felt, no words offer a definitive explanation. The mystery of life, death, and reality is something each of us has to experience and resolve, maybe again and again, within ourselves. It's not something I can ever give an answer to. Reality has to be experienced directly.

That day on the riverbank, the time came for me to go back to the retreat center for afternoon teachings. I wasn't sure if I would complete "Koan" while at Sevenoaks, but I hoped so. For now, I got up and made my trek back through the woods, the moment itself a perpetual riddle.

●

# Practice

love is patience
love is grace and
both of these are
understatements
be the mountain
be the ocean
be forgiven
be devotion

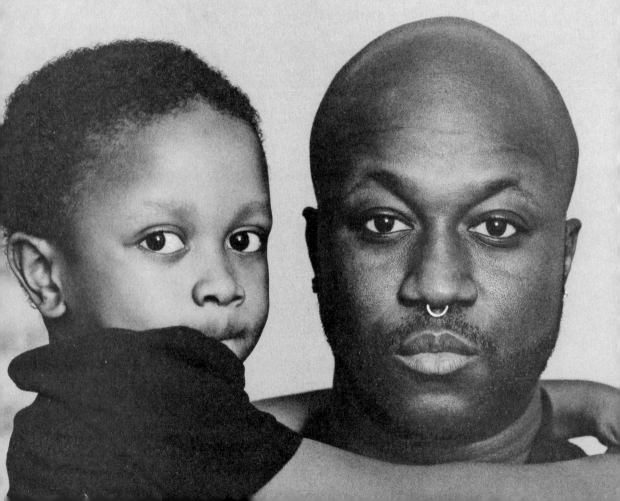

concentration
then distraction
slowly learning
self-compassion
when you feel it's
getting scary
just remember
it's temporary
first it's coming
then it's going
everything is
forever flowing
trust awareness
that's your knowing
that there's no coming
or no going
interbeing
interweaving
spring summer fall
winter speaking
staying present
then distracted
then returning
this is practice

visits by the demon
sit and watch your breathing

soon as you can see him
that's when he'll be leaving
open your awareness
let your body settle
when you learn to let go
thoughts are just an echo
let go of the struggle
let go of the striving
life is all around you
try to rest inside it
search and you won't find it when
you recognize it
God is like the sun
you are what the light is
so be the mother
be the dad
be the friend
you never had
be the sun
be the earth
be the death
be the birth
see the past
see the future
be the present
be the Buddha
when you start to
get distracted
just come back again
this is practice

# Silver Spring Diary

# CHAPTER NINE

Growing up as an African
I never felt Black enough
I'll back it up but first let me say
that feeling was
wack as fuck
a foreigner in foreign land
though I'm first-generation
my identity was more Ghanaian
than Southern plantation
product of colonization
a divided mind
further confused
by other black kids
asking if my family swung from vines
"there go the African kid
he walk funny and he talk funny

why he live out here?
I thought they got money"
found peace of mind
inside my mother's arms
crack epidemic
the 1980s broke a brothers' bond
early morning baseheads was the
friendliest
"what up young blood"

my sentiment at first was fear
but then I gave back love
niggas was nine years old
and packing heat
I was the subject of attention
for bullies and starter jacket thieves

I planned to be the one
who would survive it all
the rise and fall
not African enough for my cousins
fuck it in spite it all
the sides they don't accept me
will respect me
my silent prayer
decided willingly
to walk into the dragon's lair
couldn't be soft on that Bel Pre Street
even though my heart
was still truly the texture of fleece
I aspired to be colder
as I got a little older
then I got a little bolder

started rapping now it's over now
my niggas selling soda
open cans of Coca-Cola
selling eighths of dirt for 40
to your shorty from a rover
I went from catching the Y4
to Wheaton Plaza
to booking chicks out of the cinnabon
to caesar's palace
fast forward
and my life is suddenly
in need of balance
it's never easy
'cause a nigga like me needs a challenge
I'm just a Buddhist dude who broke the rubix cube
of what we used to do
it's Born I
allow me to reintroduce
I'm just a kid who tried to understand America
and found you had to be a gangster to make them aware of ya
and so I chose to be a gangster of love
you love yourself and love each other
then you gangster enough
peace to Silver Spring temples
silver spring malls, silver spring draws,
silver spring eight balls and silver spring gods
I paid a price so personal nobody else paid
and ever since the second grade I was self-made

I'm sick of niggas asking me if I believe in God,
you think I popped up yesterday just like a fetus?

nah

"As far as I can remember, I always wanted to be a gangster."
—**Henry Hill,** *Goodfellas*

*1989*

It's a Sunday night. My father is away at a meeting for the local Ghanaian community organization, of which he is the chairman. The Washington, DC, area is home to thousands of West African immigrants, many of them Ghanaians. Proximity to the embassy of Ghana, the ambassador, and relatives up and down the East Coast have made DC a growing hub for immigrants from the country formerly known as the Gold Coast seeking a new life in America.

My parents were both born in Ghana; they met in the United States. My father was born in the capital city of Accra and my mother was born in the mountains of Koforidua. They both came from prominent families, although culturally they were different in significant ways. For one, my parents are from two different tribes. My mother is an Akan, and my father is a Ga-Adangbe. My mother's language, Twi, and my father's language, Ga, could not be more different, at least to my ears. Due to living in the capital, my father's family had been adjacent to the culture of the British colonial system that had infiltrated and dug its claws into Ghana for hundreds of years. My mother's family, far removed from the capital city, maintained a way of life that was, while modern, more closely aligned with the old, pre-colonial ways.

This Sunday night in 1989, my mother and I sit on the couch in our small townhouse in Silver Spring, Maryland, just off Bel Pre Road. Our street, Astrodome Drive, isn't poor, but it isn't rich either. Some of the houses in our neighborhood are subsidized, inhabited by families living on government assistance. The general area along Bel Pre Road is plagued with sporadic home break-ins and the ravages of the crack epidemic that has swept the region. My house, however, is a sanctuary. My parents are afforded deep respect by our neighbors, many of whom—especially those he has helped in his role as a legal specialist and child support social worker—view my father as a hero. He has helped mothers in our community support their children and children's fathers stay out of jail so both parents can amicably care for their kids. My mother is an event planner and executive assistant; though she never went to college, her intelligence, determination, and personality have given her opportunities many people of color, and people in general, could only dream of.

With my father away at a meeting, the atmosphere in the house is relaxed. Just me and my mom—the luxury of being an only child. Al Pacino is on the television as Michael Corleone, burning two holes through the screen with the icy heat of his commanding, silent glare. I'm too young to really understand, but I take cues from my mom, who sits and watches, rapt. Every once in a while, she makes a comment: "Al Pacino is an incredible actor." "This movie is so powerful."

Even at this young age I've already watched *The Godfather* countless times, sometimes with my mom, sometimes by myself, sometimes with friends. More and more, I've identified with and idolize the character of Michael Corleone. He is, like me, the prized son of immigrants who struggled to make a living in America and stayed close to their insular community even once they succeeded. Like me, Michael is loved by his parents but perceived by his contemporaries as different at best and weak at worst.

*the sides that don't accept me, will respect me.*

The next morning, I'm awakened by the sound of my alarm clock blurting out inspirational messages from an action hero. My mother has laid out an outfit for me, a matching shirt and shorts set, golden yellow with an all-over print of Ghanaian *adinkra* symbols. I wolf down my cereal, hug my parents goodbye, and begin to walk to the neighborhood bus stop. Along the way I see grown-ups with restless eyes full of lightning, darkness, hunger, and intensity. Victims of addiction— we used to call them *crackheads*. Their stares are alarming, sometimes frightening, until one of them cracks a big smile and reveals a missing tooth as he waves at me, saying, "Have a good one today, Youngblood." "Thank you! You too," I respond.

I keep walking, the bus stop comes into view, and I see many of the respected, popular kids from the adjacent, rougher neighborhoods already there. One of them spots me from a distance. "Ay, look at Oom-FuFu walking up here with that funny African shit on!" Everybody laughs, some make Tarzan noises. My stomach drops. I want to disappear.

I sit alone on the bus, knowing that at school there will be more intentional and unintentional mispronunciations of my name, there will be more jokes about my outfit. There will be more....

The weekend rolls around again. I've endured another week at school. Every time I come home and my parents ask me how my day was, I just answer, "Fine." I don't tell them about the constant bullying and harassment, don't tell them I was jumped by some of the kids after school one day for standing up for myself, or that I wake up dreading the reality that awaits me at school.

This weekend, my parents and I have been invited to some kind of function—somebody was born, somebody died, somebody graduated, or somebody got married; since everyone in the community was considered family, nearly every event required our presence. On the day of the event, we dress in beautiful Ghanaian regalia: flowing embroidered gowns, beautiful prints, and immaculate headwear. Knowing I will be around others like me, I am comfortable in my clothes. We arrive, and my father receives an introduction before taking over the microphone to greet all the attendees. He and my mother sit at the high table, reserved for guests of honor and revered members of the community. I look out for the

# Not Black enough for Black Americans.

# Not African enough for Black Africans.

# I was an island unto myself.

usual friends and "cousins," and we smile when our eyes find each other. We laugh and joke in ways only us immigrant kids can understand, and for a time, I am at ease.

The night wears on, the young people settle down. Conversations begin to slip in and out of English and into either pidgin or Ga, neither of which I can speak. "Ofosu, you don't understand?" "No," I say, embarrassed. "I don't speak it." My friends and the other kids laugh. I can feel them talking about me without understanding the words. Conversations continue, and now I sit at the table feeling surrounded but alone. For me, my bonding over the pressures and realities of our similar upbringings could only go so far—since my parents were from different tribes and could only communicate with each other in English, I was the only one who couldn't easily slip into a different language or joke in pidgin. Part of me was not African enough for the African kids. I sip ginger ale and get lost in my imagination, reciting song lyrics I heard at my next-door neighbor's house. Rap music is like a puzzle, I think, so interesting how all the words fit together and deliver a concept in rhyme. It's like poetry.... My father's hand on my shoulder interrupts my thoughts—it's time to go.

At school and to the wider public, the distinction between being African and Black American didn't exist. To the general population, I was simply Black. My father, a Pan-Africanist, preached to me that all Black people are one family, all around the world. This was the philosophy of Ghana's liberator, Kwame Nkrumah, to whom my father was ideologically devoted. I carried this notion in my heart. *All Black people are one.* At school, however, the human propensity to make painful divisions became more and more invasive. At the most basic level, my name was strange; my seemingly simple name, "Ofosu," didn't roll off anyone's tongue easily and was often the subject of brutal jokes and purposeful mispronunciations.

Walking to the bus stop some mornings, I wore outfits gifted to me by relatives in Ghana—beautiful colors and prints very different from what American kids wore. I sometimes walked to the bus stop in tears, knowing the ridicule would come. Even my English was different. Informed more by my parents' beautiful command of their colonial inheritance but without the nuances of American, specifically Black American, intonations or slang, my way of speaking was "too white."

Along with other cruel nicknames, I earned the dubious distinction of being a completely anomalous contradiction: an African white boy. Not Black enough for Black Americans. Not African enough for Black Africans. I was an island unto myself.

As high school rolls around, I sense the impossibility of any sort of organic belonging. Fueled by comic books and loneliness, I tell my parents I want to join the military, become a navy SEAL—if I can't find belonging organically, perhaps I can belong to something inorganic but strong, somewhere I won't be alone. Fearing I might enlist, my parents find a military school for me to attend that will put me on the path to going to one of the various military academies. Now, every morning before classes at St. John's College High School in Washington, DC, I put on a military uniform: a light green shirt, dark green pants, black patent leather shoes, black tie, and a gold tie clip with my school's initials on them. My mother drives me to school. We carpool, and each morning we pick up a Bolivian American kid named John Lujan who quietly gets into the backseat and says nothing, his eyes covered by thick, dark bangs that remain motionless no matter what I play on the radio.

I find solace and purpose in the militarized way of life and way of thinking. It doesn't take much effort to find belonging in this type of culture. I begin to relax, to resign myself: this will be my life. We practice real army drills in the woods after school. Months pass, and I join the elite team of JROTC students, the Raiders. One morning when we pick John up on the way to school, his attitude is a little different. He speaks to us, says good morning. He seems more awake, more present. I turn on the radio and nod my head to whatever the mainstream has to offer that morning. As we pull up to the entrance of St. John's and get out of the car, John pulls a cassette tape out of his pocket and hands it to me. "Here," he says. "If we're gonna ride in the car together every day, you're gonna have to listen to better music." This is the most John has spoken to me since the start of school months ago. I am both honored and stunned. I look at the cassette tape and see John has annotated the inner flap with the names of each artist and song. Some names I recognize, some names I don't: Wu-Tang Clan, Nas, the Notorious B.I.G., Mobb Deep, Black Moon, Jeru the Damajah, Smif-N-Wessun, Group Home, Gangstarr.

I go home that afternoon, put the tape into my stereo, and press play. Within the first minute, I experience something like a spiritual epiphany. All these rappers are talking to me, sharing their pain with me—their own loneliness, the wisdom acquired through suffering, their ambition, their defiance, their own personal militancy, their humanity. I finally feel that I am truly not alone. I listen to the tape over and over, absorbing the words and sounds. There are even samples of Al Pacino movies, important lines from *The Godfather, Scarface, Carlitos's Way*. There is profanity and tales of criminality, explanations of what it means to be a gangster, what it means to be Black in America, and how there is divinity in our Blackness.

This tape becomes my obsession and my education, John my professor and true friend. I am a little behind the curve on the 90s East Coast hip-hop revival, but I quickly catch up. John and I spend weekends together listening to songs from established voices and new up-and-comers in the underground; we decipher their lyrics, their choice of beats, make meaning out of all of it, and relate our own lives to theirs. After a while, it isn't enough to simply be a consumer of hip-hop: I have to be a part of it.

The shopping malls in Silver Spring are proving grounds for all the local rappers. Food courts in the mall hum loudly with the sound of hands drumming on tables as MCs face each other in battle, aiming to defeat one another in a war of spontaneous words—freestyling. To step into the cipher, the ring, you can't be timid or afraid. You have to be ready. If you aren't skilled enough to enter the cipher, you could very well face physical harm from people there to seriously hone their craft. I begin spending my after-school time and weekends here, and I make friends. I become a part of something. I belong. My friends are Black, white, and Latino. The artform becomes our religion.

Some of my new friends are first-generation Americans like me, and we commiserate over our parents' fear of and disdain for hip-hop. Some of my friends are from lower economic backgrounds, some sell drugs, some live lives that parallel the songs we listen to. I learn from them what it means to be bold, what it means to be strong. Even though they might be frightening to civilians, I see the good heart in each of these soldiers. This will be my family. This will be my life.

My military ambitions completely fade away. I complete high school, but my singular focus is music. I start my own rap group, the Last Day Apostles, and we make spiritual, densely lyrical hip-hop reminiscent of Wu-Tang Clan, KillArmy, and the Gravediggaz. We are an unstoppable force in the underground battle circuit. Against my parents' wishes, I continue to follow my musical ambitions in college at American University (AU). My roommate came to AU to study music production and I see this coincidence as no coincidence at all, but divine providence. We build a recording studio in our dorm room, and it becomes the hub for new artists all across the DC area to cut their first demos—Leonard Hall room 626 becomes legendary. I barely go to class. To fund the studio and support my friends, I connect with a "connect" and begin selling large amounts of marijuana on campus. Slowly but surely, I become affiliated with a criminal way of life, associating with people my parents would never want me to but finding family, friendship, strength, and protection in the process. More than that, I find humanity. I find commonality. We all feel lost and alone, all share a longing for meaning and connection, no matter what tribe we belong to. I meet my future wife, Ayanna, I meet my musical family, and I am never alone again.

Close brushes with the law, friends getting shot, and my own desire to be true to who I really am inside eventually lead me to leave selling drugs behind and embrace a more spiritual way of life. My unique story isn't actually that unique; through the reality of not being attached to one particular identity, I find freedom in connecting with all types of people from all types of backgrounds. The diverse identities in me that used to be a source of deep pain become my treasure.

As far back as I can remember, I always wanted to be a gangster. What is a gangster? I tell my children a gangster is a liberated person— anyone who lives by their own code and vision and doesn't allow society to define who they are. America is a country of gangsters. I choose to be a gangster of love, to love unconditionally—defiantly, if needed. Hip-hop awakened me.

La Cosa Nostra. This thing of ours.

# Avalo

# CHAPTER TEN

Avalokiteshvara
while practicing deeply
with the insight that brings us
to the other shore
suddenly discovered that
all of the five *skandhas*
are equally empty
and with this realization
he overcame all ill-being

words are prison
blur my vision
her position
perfect wisdom
I've been sitting
digging deeper
you can see the
*muchalinda*
intravenous
inner demons
in between us
while I'm breathing
I've been dreaming
I've been seeking
hibernation
I was sleeping
she's been waking
she's been taking
flights to Venus
ain't no faking
like Siddhartha
meeting Mara
like Avalo-
kitesh-vara
put your guard down
keep your heart up
only love can
keep the stars up
like Siddhartha
meeting Mara

like Avalo-
kitesh-vara

all of my fear and my pain
breath breath breath
all my regret and my shame
breath
callin' my ancestors names
breath breath breath
we are both one and the same
breath

stop and listen
water glistens
I'm adrift in
contradictions
my reflection
intersection
of living reckless
and introspection
I sit on the floor
look at my feelings and more
but while I'm healing
I can't help but feeling
I'm still being torn
maybe I'm being reborn
maybe I'm still being formed
maybe the "I" I call myself
is really the eye of the storm
tell me my mind isn't gone
tell me I'm writing my wrongs

tell me it matters
whenever we gather
to write a new song
she's been waking
she's been taking
flights to Venus
ain't no faking
like Siddhartha
meeting Mara
like Avalo-
kitesh-vara
put your guard down
keep your heart up
only love can
keep the stars up
like the Buddha
meeting Mara
like Avalo
kitesh vara
like Siddhartha
in the garden
like Avalo-
kitesh-vara

oh my beloved one
my inner child
I know that you are afraid
I know how much you hurt
how much it hurts every day
I know your wish
your wish to be free

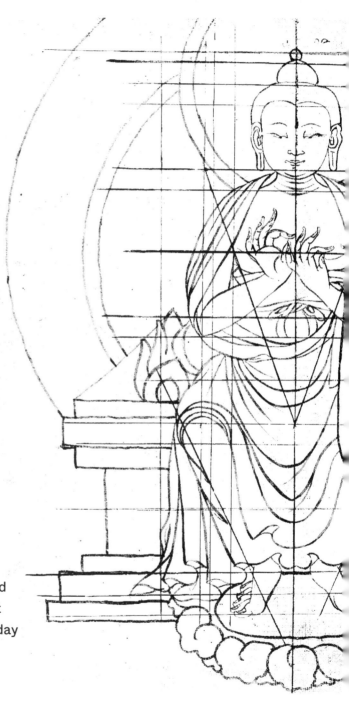

your wish to be healed
walk with me and I will help you find your way
I want you to know
that everything is okay
the things that happened to you
weren't your fault
you don't have to hurt yourself
because of them
I want you to remember
to be gentle to yourself
to love yourself
as if you were your own precious child
beloved one
there is nothing to be afraid of
look around you
the entire world
the entire cosmos
is who you are
the wind, the clouds
the flowers, the storms
the love, the agony
all of it is you
you are already free
you are already
exactly who you want to be
look inside and see yourself
inside you is an ocean
of love and understanding
look inside you
and you will find
the bodhisattva
Avalokiteshvara

"Avalo" on a coffee run to Dunkin' Donuts. Listening to the beat, produced by my friend Daniel Andres Rodriguez Correter (DaRC Music), on my morning coffee drive, I entered a different dimension: a space of deep feeling, saturated with hues of blackness and gold, flowing rivers of purple, and a sky full of jewels. It was as though I was listening to the sound of compassion itself, experiencing its ability to recognize, accept fully, comfort, and heal.

All these qualities—and more—are associated with the *bodhisattva* (enlightened being) Avalokiteshvara, the embodiment of compassion. The name Avalokiteshvara means "the one who hears the cries of the world" and points to compassion's all-encompassing, all-embracing quality. The bodhisattva of compassion is known around the world by many names. Neither definitively male or female, Avalokiteshvara is also known as Kwan Yin, Chenrezig, Kannon, and Quan Thế Âm, to name a few. Compassion is so fundamental to the Buddhist path that it came to be personified in an archetypal being, one who reaches out in the never-ending task of meeting the pain of all beings. In the ultimate sense, Avalokiteshvara is the compassionate nature in each one of us. Whenever our hearts, minds, words, and actions reach out to embrace any being, including ourselves, with lovingkindness, presence, or understanding, Avalokiteshvara is there.

I strongly believe that my children—Sundara, Samadhi, Sati, and Siddhattha—rode the energy of Avalokiteshvara into this world. They bear the mark of Avalokiteshvara on their hearts. In my eyes, my children are divine beings. I've spent many nights bowing at their feet while they sleep. I believe my role as their father is to not only nurture and protect them, but to continue to remind them that they are Avalokiteshvara themselves. I try not to do this in a heavy-handed way, but just by encouraging them to see the world through eyes of compassion. Being their father has taught me the meaning of grace and unconditional love and has given my life purpose. Being their father has also awoken latent traumas within me that I didn't know or had forgotten were there as well as bringing forth unimaginable anxieties and feelings of shame and inadequacy.

I often feel far away from my mission to guide my children back to themselves, to their true nature, as I fumble through my own life. During my struggles, I've come to realize that self-compassion is the beginning of everything. Learning to accept myself, offer myself grace, and be humbled by my own shortcomings makes it difficult for me to find unforgivable flaws in others. What is in me is in others, and what is in others is in me. Compassion for myself is the beginning of compassion for all. I bow to the bodhisattva Avalokiteshvara for this life-saving understanding.

My wife, Ayanna, and my daughter Sundara are featured on "Avalo," which begins with the opening lines of the Heart Sutra as translated by Thích Nhất Hạnh. Written over 1,300 years ago, the Heart Sutra points us to understanding the nature of reality and our place in it. In the Sutra, Avalokiteshvara shares that understanding who and what we really are is the key to spiritual liberation.

I first read the Heart Sutra over a decade ago in Baltimore while on a Greyhound bus to a nightclub where I was about to perform. As I read the words "form is emptiness, emptiness is form," something indescribable happened. It was as if lightning struck me. Looking up from the book, I felt like Neo in the Matrix when he saw the code behind the programming of his world. For days, I saw everything with new eyes. I could feel that I and everyone, every creature I encountered, was free and expansive, not bound by our forms, feelings, or perceptions. I felt wide awake and electric. I wondered if this was some kind of permanent shift of awakening, but it turned out to be more like a glimpse behind the curtain. Eventually, my habitual thoughts, actions, and words crept back in. Still, I had witnessed something—the endless openness of the sky within each of us.

It's fitting that my wife's voice is the first voice on "Avalo," since the first verse is really about her. Since I met Ayanna, I've regarded her as a person who is truly "awake"—wisdom and compassion seem to flow effortlessly through her. Taught by her mother, Suzanne Anderson—a powerful meditation teacher—Ayanna has practiced meditation since childhood. I often feel both deeply spiritually connected to Ayanna and also as if she is light years beyond my comprehension. Thầy says to think of the sun, the ultimate source of life and vitality on our planet, as our own heart. Ayanna is the sun in my heart.

"Avalo" is a conversation between spirit and flesh, ideal and actual, relative and ultimate. My wife and children represent the ultimate to me. I often feel as though I'm circling in the cul-de-sac of the mundane, trying to reach them. At the same time, we are all together, woven tightly, threads in a tapestry I can feel but can't fully see. There is always an element of mystery. We are held together by ancestors of spirit and flesh. If we ever find ourselves lost, we know we can come home.

Healing from trauma, overcoming fear, learning to begin again after failing—as a partner, a parent, a practitioner, a person—all of it can be so hard. The child within each of us needs love, compassion, reassurance, and a reminder that we are not separate from anything— from ourselves, from other beings, or from the world itself. There is nothing to fear. Freedom—change, flow, and openness—is who we are. The closing monologue on "Avalo" felt more channeled than written. Ayanna and Sundara, mother and daughter, speak together to the inner child of the ultimate reality—each one of us. When these words came through me, I needed them desperately. The Dharma came to my rescue from within, pouring the love I couldn't live without back into me.

# What is in me is in others, and what is in others is in me.

# Compassion for myself is the beginning of compassion for all.

*the wind, the clouds,*
*the flowers, the storms,*
*the love, the agony,*
*all of it is you*
*you are already free*
*you are already*
*exactly who you want to be*
*look inside and see yourself*
*inside you is an ocean*
*of love and understanding*
*look inside you*
*and you will find the bodhisattva*
*Avalokiteshvara*

# Ayanna

words can't describe
what I saw in you
I approached without a plan,
never thought it through
all I wanted was for us to be connected
asked if I could take you out to dinner
you accepted

I told you I was a SEAL
in the Lord's Navy
you told me you was the same
we was both crazy
your mother taught you how to meditate
so did mine
and you grew up a little too fast
so did I
couldn't understand the feeling
this is more than love
it's like the atom split
that found a fit
in both of us
you and I
the story of the
wolf and dove
your shoulders held
all of my tears
as I opened up
half Pittsburgh
half Atlanta
Silver Spring
taught me
it's the little things
that matter
your parents' one and only
my parents' one and only
until the day we found each other
both of us were lonely

I was 18
you was 19
young lovers but it's more than it might seem
this the bodhisattva path
this is Mahakala
this is Kwan yin

Avalokiteshvara
this is gods' wisdom
this is psalms written
this is the Bhagavad Gita
to free the heart's prison
they said you never talk
they felt awkwardly
I just looked at them
and smiled and said
she talks to me
your face can only be compared
to the rising sun
I pray to be the nest
where you rest
when your flyin's done
I just hope you know
I worship you
and when we reincarnate,
I'm gonna search for you

I never want to be away from you
wake up in the morning
and I pray for you
they say the Dharma is a sacred jewel
when they ask me what the Dharma is
I say it's you
before it ever was a song
we called each other twin
last lifetime in the temple
now we back again
thank you for your wisdom

all the life you've given
thank you for your sense of humor
thank you for existing
I know I still have work to do
you're the reason life is purposeful
I just hope you know I worship you
and when we reincarnate
I'm gonna search for you
but for now
time found us
and my gratitude is boundless

# CHAPTER TWELVE

# Life of the Buddha Part 1

once upon a time
there was the prince who was promised
who was born under a full moon
and gifted with knowledge
even the prophets
and the scriptures acknowledged
that he would either rule the world
or free the children from bondage
son of a king with the blood of a warrior
wisdom was his convoy
love was his courier
Maya and Bimbisara
holy mama and papa
manifested their dreaming
and so they named him Siddhartha
every wish is fulfilled
what does the motivation
underneath our wishes reveal?
every now and then
something in him would feel
like the world isn't real
like a gerbil in wheel
sex money and power
women for every hour
rare wine to pair with
the dinners that he devoured
but all it made him feel was emptiness
had an idea to turn his crib
into an empty nest

so he left the palace walls
so he could learn about it all
if everything was bull
then he would learn to be the matador
probably had second thoughts
probably missed his fam of course
deep in the jungle
thinking he went about it wrong
still he went to teacher after teacher
in the forest practicing
with seeker after seeker
studied with Alara Kalama
taught him meditative absorption
that's known as the Jhanas
but when Alara taught Siddhartha
all that he could teach him
he saw the student has surpassed him
and he couldn't reach him
so off Siddhartha went
to find another tutor
and found himself at the feet of
Uddaka Ranmputra
Uddaka taught him how to reach
the highest state of mind
but it didn't give the satisfaction
that he came to find
Siddhartha tried to find a way
to go beyond himself
so he sat under a tree
and he starved himself

first he gave up his wealth
then he gave up his health
is this what he was searching for
leaving his family
to only end up hurting more
and just before he slipped away
he thought about a middle way
Siddhartha took some food that was offered
and found the strength to meditate
a little bit longer
the devil and his army
rose up to stop him
brought women to seduce him
and demons to haunt him
but nothing could disturb his composure
and the earth began to fill with the smell of ambrosia
enlightenment was more than dreams he invented
and the first thing he saw was
everything is connected
and so compassion is the truth from the get-go
and you can only achieve satisfaction if you let go

# How Many Times

how many times

did this like how many times

how many lines

did it like how many lines

how many dimes

did it like how many dimes

how many climbs

climbing up how many climbs

how many words

did it like how many words

I went berserk

did it 'til I went berserk

I put in work

put it in put it in work

I put in work

put it in put it in work

kundalini rising up in me
when u niggas ask what's up with me
conversation is a luxury
but it's really not my cup of tea
I've been talking to my spirit guides
I've been talking to my spirit guides
and I tell 'em what I feel inside
try to see it with the clearest eyes
complicated when you still a thug
hard to fake it if it isn't love
love the fame but it's still a drug
meditation is real enough
talking through sacred geometry
words are my favorite artistry

mama I made it for all to see
my life is more like an odyssey
stimulated pineal gland
come together like sea and sand
look inside 'til I see the plan
or I die and repeat again
Europeans was fooling us
I've been breathing with Buddhist monks
Europeans was ruling us
now I'm free but my mood is fucked
I'm not seeking no validation
when I speak it's a fashion statement
get my people up out the matrix
I'm like Neo with blacker faces
om mani padme hum
om mani padme hum
when I'm reciting my prayers tho'
I'm taking calls from the jail
every morning
and when we hang up
I just pray for bro

how many times
did this like how many times ...

do what I needed
and they just repeat it
I'm still undefeated
and they can't believe it
I serve it you eat it
my cipher completed
my life in my lyrics ignited your speakers
chop the top off a couple coups
lots of love for my brother Toof
lots of love for my brother Waze
meditation for a hundred days
talking more with my brother Mac
hustle forward don't hustle back
AB Logic my brother Nate
kept it honest and wasn't
fake
my life is more than a story
AJ Adriana and Cory
my wife and my kids and my family
those the ones that protected my sanity

how many times
did this like how many times...

My alarm rings: morning is here. My body feels the presence of one of my children in our bed, sandwiched between my wife and me. My eyes still closed, I reach over and lay a hand on their little ankle. *At what point in the night did they come into the room to snuggle up between us?* My mind dances lazily between lament and nostalgia, both centered on the question "How many times?" or more accurately, "How many *more* times?" Part of me wonders how many more times we will allow this little one to sneak into our bed at night when we've been encouraging them to sleep through the night in their own bed. Part of me imagines a future when they will be too grown, perhaps too far away with families of their own, to crawl into our bed again.

Suddenly, my thoughts turn away from the child in our bed and toward a sense of dread and foreboding. My muscles tighten, waves of heat cascade through my body, and my heart rate rises in a dull, sick panic. *I am afraid.* Afraid of the hell my mind will put me through today. I sense a familiar, relentless cycle of horrible, intrusive thoughts followed by deep shame followed by moments of recovery followed by a state of anxiety and fear about the next wave of thoughts on the horizon. As much as I want to put on a brave face, as much as *I will* put on a brave face, I know my torture is about to begin. *How many times?* How many times will I experience the devastating grip of this mysterious condition? How many times do I have to deal with this? What did I do to deserve this? I'm not a bad person, but my intrusive thoughts constantly scream at me and project terrible images in my mind that try to convince me otherwise. *How many times will this go on?*

I couldn't tell you when exactly this memory took place. It could have been any morning in my life these last twenty years. Only recently have I finally received a diagnosis and treatment for a particular kind of obsessive-compulsive disorder often referred to as "Pure O." This type of OCD expresses itself through distressing mental obsessions and intrusive thoughts and is often brought on by childhood and young adult traumas.

That morning, I get out of bed quietly and walk to the altar in my meditation room. I arrange my cushion and sit, pulling my right foot up over my left thigh in the half lotus position. Resting my hands in my lap, I bring my attention to my breathing and watch the rise and fall of each breath in my abdomen as I've been taught. At first, I feel wonderful—grateful for this practice, grateful for an escape from the fear I had just been feeling, grateful to be a student of the Buddha, a student of my teacher, and a practitioner on the path. I notice my breathing: the thousands of micro-moments in each inhale and exhale, the way life and death happen billions of times within a single breath cycle. My embodied experience of impermanence verifies the Buddha's teachings. I feel warm, at peace.

Then, slowly at first, a sick feeling invades the pit of my stomach, a squeezing and tightening begins on the left side of my head, an ache seeps into my hands, and discomfort spreads throughout my body. Anxiety curls its fingers around me as I brace for the cycle of intrusive thoughts and visceral shame. All joy and ease leaves my body; only terror and dread remain. I try to breathe through it, but things become darker and darker as the worst possible thoughts enter my mind, devastating me. I feel ashamed. Angry at myself. Perhaps I even strike myself. I feel so far away from the path, so sad and exhausted. I cry. I find my way back to my breath, console myself, I try to reason with my mind. I try to replace all the negative thoughts with thoughts of loving kindness. Mostly though, I remain dejected and angry. Ashamed and exhausted. The bell rings—7:30 a.m., the end of meditation. I put on a brave face. *How many times?*

*Sometime in the past …*

It's evening. Nightlife in Washington, DC, is about to begin. It's time for me to head into the city either for a performance or a meeting or simply to be seen. It's all part of being a rapper on the rise in the nation's capital. It's important to be seen at night, it's important to walk in the club without waiting in line, for the promoters to sit you at a prominent table, for the gangsters to love you, for the women to love you, for the people to envy you, for the DJ to play your songs and shout your name when you walk into the building. *It's important*, I tell myself every night as I put on my "Born I" uniform and leave my family behind to go play this game that hopefully will lead to my success, our success. *It's important*, I tell myself, my wife, my kids, for me to be out, maybe until 10:00 the next morning, because it means I spent time with important people, had important conversations, advanced my career, secured investments, raised my profile.

I hit the city, either by myself, with my manager Nate, or with an entourage. Either way, wherever I go I'm treated with love and respect. I don't wait in line, neither do my friends—we are treated like important people by important people in the city. I tell myself it's hard to earn this kind of love and respect from important people, gatekeepers, in a political town like DC. It's taken a lot of time. A new single of mine has come out, and when I slide into the club, the DJ plays it immediately and announces I'm in the building. All of it makes me exhausted and anxious. I mask it with a smile and prayer hands. For the entire day I've been hanging on by a thread, battling this OCD condition. I'm tired, I don't feel important, I don't feel special; I feel small, sad,

and depressed. If I'm gonna make it through the night, I'm going to need vodka. Lots and lots of vodka. Swimming in a river of vodka, I can cross the river of social anxiety and depression. I smile; I make jokes; I hold court; I'm the life of the party.

The club shuts down, and some of the most important people in the city invite us to an afterparty. *This is important*, I tell myself. This is why we came out in the first place. At the afterparty, the host plays my music, talks to me about my vision, invests in my work. Everyone has had a lot to drink, it's time to "even out" a bit—someone calls a dealer and soon we're surrounded by plates full of cocaine. Conversations continue until the sun comes up, a nonverbal queue for all of us vampires to retreat to our homes. I drive home feeling I've made major progress, but as the alcohol and drugs begin to wear off, I'm no longer sure. I begin to question if all this time and energy is worth it. I begin to regret reckless things I said under the influence. I regret being away from home for so long for something so ambiguous. In the comedown, shame triggers a new cycle of horrible, intrusive thoughts exacerbated by the lack of serotonin in my brain after the drugs used it all up. As I open the door to my house and walk in, relief mixed

the unenlightened
spend lifetime
after lifetime
wandering around
the wheel of
deluded existence

We spend our
precious energy
on the
achievement of
the ephemeral.

with misery washes over me. *How many times?*

In Buddhist cosmology, it is said that the unenlightened spend lifetime after lifetime wandering around the wheel of deluded existence: *samsara*. Driven by our ignorance, we act through greed, hatred, and delusion and create causes, conditions, and effects that bind us to an endless round of birth, death, and rebirth. In this cycle, we are disconnected from the true nature of reality and chase after only our basic needs and fleeting, illusory desires. We spend our precious energy on the achievement of the ephemeral. "How Many Times?" is, in part, a meditation on my experience of samsara within samsara, on the cycles and habits that often have felt impossible to break. Without the practice of self-compassion, the support and forgiveness of my family and friends, and guidance from wise teachers, therapists, and my parents, I don't know if I would be alive today. His Holiness the Dalai Lama has said, "If you want to know what your past life was like, look at your life right now; if you want to know what your future life will be like, look at your life right now."

My life has been a mix of wholesome and unwholesome, sacred and profane, peace and violence, joy beyond words and sadness beyond comprehension. "How Many Times?" tries to make sense of it all, to see where my compass points on the wheel of samsara: Am I awakening? Am I falling deeper into delusion? What has all this truly been for? What have I accomplished that is meaningful? Every moment I spend my life energy; every moment the grains in the hourglass of my life deplete. What am I doing? How can I be both the hero and the villain in my own story? Both the victim and savior? Am I just spinning my wheels? *How many times?* Hundreds? Thousands? Billions?

The Zen teacher Rev. angel Kyodo williams has said "enough" is the most adult word in the English language. This teaching has a special significance for me—the words "you are enough" have become very important in my life, work, and practice. How long does it take to arrive at "enough"? What does it mean to be enough? Sometimes I arrive at the place of "enough" and encounter a new vista, new ground from which to see and interact with the world—a new space. Sometimes being enough is just out of my reach and I enter the spin cycle again. I keep exploring, keep trying, keep writing songs. I come back to my cushion, to music, to the koan: What does it mean to be enough?

*Today ...*

I'm in Derby, Indiana in the dining hall of a rustic campground. It's after 10 p.m. Tomorrow I will begin co-teaching a weeklong meditation retreat for teenagers. It's meaningful, powerful work, and I see how all my struggles have made it possible for me to do it from the heart so I can hopefully be of benefit to others when I share how meditation, self-compassion, support from loving people, and simply not giving up on myself have allowed me to be alive today.

Tonight, I think of new songs to write. My practice has changed significantly since I began receiving treatment for my OCD and adapting my approach to meditation. Lately I've been sitting with much more joy and ease, allowing my experience to be whatever it is from moment to moment and relaxing into the spaciousness of my mind, my body, and this life. I often feel no point at which the external world ends and my internal world begins. I feel grateful, so grateful, to be here. I see sacredness and vastness in

everything. Honestly, sometimes it's too much for my "small self" to bear, and I'm encouraged to embody what Suzuki Roshi calls "Big Mind." My practice is not a search for becoming, but an expression of what I already am. Each time I sit, I make peace with vastness.

*How can I express this in a song?* New music asks to be born. I know this feeling: brand new, healed in so many ways, yet with more work to be done. I know my music will reflect this; I don't yet know how. Although I am new in this moment, I've been on this journey before. The bodhisattva vow is forever. "How Many Times?" is a hundred koans in one.

# CHAPTER FOURTEEN

# Love Is Patience

autumn leaves escape the tree of life
instead of speaking two and thrice
I try to be precise
often I end where I begin at
it's cyclical
more like elliptical
within the synapse
where I been at
the temple or my house
staring at my children

sentimental with my spouse
I thought I wasn't strong enough
to go a better route
so I'm thanking Mahakala
for the strength that got me out
concentrated pleasures
simplicity from letting go
of complicated measures
my heart betrays the soft embrace
of Dharma when I'm sped up
truth is that I'm never gonna change
'til I'm fed up
'til then I keep my head up,
quietly staring at the wall
observe the present moment
while I'm bearing all my flaws
who knew that my awareness

would be tearing down the walls
of my carelessness
until I learned to care about it all

love is patience

existing in a state of grace is humility
Shakyamuni said embrace your ability
sitting with my master
the blaze of her scrutiny
nothing could taste more beautifully
I used to speak with food in cheek
when truth was weak and youth was bleak
but somehow I still grew to seek
the Buddha's speech for true relief
happiness is new to me
laughing as it grew in me
my teachers words
and how I seek to serve
needed congruency
I fought a war inside
that probably made Jehovah close his eyes
and meditate on ways to help me
find a path to open skies
and from the peace revealed to me
what remains is still to see
for now where does my stillness lead?
bowing at my children's feet

patience

love is patience

# Sunyata

I am the sword and the sheath
I am the wolf and the sheep
I am the fire and snow
I am the cold in the heat
I am the soldier who weeps
I am the stone when it speaks
I am the heart of the beggar
who enters the soul of the thief
I am the king and the queen
I am the prince and his team
I am the princess who doesn't have interest
in all of the schemes
I am the eagle and fish
I am the dream and the wish
I am asleep and adrift
I am as free as the wind
I am awakening mind
I am forsaken in time
I am upgraded in rhyme
I am just taking my time
sometimes I speak out of turn
sometimes I bleed and I burn
sometimes I totally die
sometimes you see me return
I am the blade and the wrist
I am the space and the ship

# CHAPTER FIFTEEN

I am both heaven and hell
I just decided to sit
I am the emptiest form
I am connected and torn
so-called perfectionist yeah
because I am the messiest born
I am the yin and the yang
I am the click and the bang
I am the ship when it sank
I am the river and bank
I am not holding a grudge
I am the lotus in mud
I was alone in my pain
I am just getting unstuck
I lift my heart up to God
I become one with stars
I bow to the Buddha
who told me the truth that
it's all a mirage
I am no birth and no death
I am the person who wept
I am earth, fire, and water
and space as I nurture my breath
I am my mom and my dad
I am a song when it's sad
I am the joy of a child
I am King Kong when he's mad
I am no death and no birth
I am the pleasure and hurt
one day we all will be free
one day I'll never return
I am the joy of the crow

I am the boy when he knows
I am the girl when she thinks
I am the world at a blink
God is in all of my cells
God knows that I've been through hell
nothing compared to what I
put the people I love through as well
every new breath is a chance
every new step is a dance
you are not walking alone
see the footprints in the sand
I have no reason to doubt
I feel my feet on the ground
only way out is within
I sit and breathe in and out
don't get the blues when it's tough
don't be confused when it's rough
I wrote this song just to help you
remember that you are enough

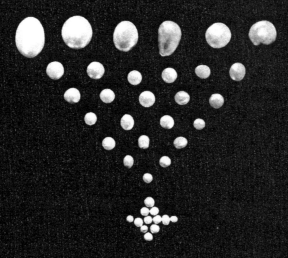

I sit in the kneeling *seiza* posture for meditation. My hands rest on the top of my thighs, my right hand cradled in the left, my thumbs coming together to form the cosmic mudra. I look out the window, watching the mighty oak and pine tree dance in the wind and rain. The periphery of a tropical storm is crossing over the skies in Maryland where I live. Pinecones are soaked to a brownish purple, oak leaves, still on branches, are flipped over by the unforgiving whipping winds. I sit and look out.

My gaze lowers, taking in the small altar in front of me, the reddish-brown bodhi seed prayer beads resting between a reddish-brown statue of Thích Nhất Hạnh and a statuette of Batman. A picture of Padmasambhava. My eyes begin to close.

I open my ears: the sound of rain and wind is more gentle than its visible activity. Ayanna's footsteps enter the soundscape, accented by the jingle of car keys in her hand or pocket. I relax, slowly drawing my attention inward.

I scan awareness through my body. My lower back calls out, says, "Here, there is tremendous pain." Like streaks of lightning shooting across the night sky, pain cuts through my lower back and hips with sharp, serrated slashes. I've been passing a kidney stone for days, and the pain has been unbearable. A visit to the hospital, medication, and rest have been helpful. Today I felt strong enough to sit.

I continue to scan my body. Though it is the loudest, pain is not the only experience happening here. In my arms there is silence, peace, neutrality. In my head there is some tightness on the left side, an OCD pattern I am familiar with. On the right side, there is ease. In my thighs there is stability and silence, like the trunk of the oak tree outside. In my chest and abdomen there is movement. The rising and settling of each breath is enjoyable for a few moments, but as each breath deepens, my torso expands and activates the pain in my back and hips. For some reason, I smile.

Thoughts arise: *When will I get better? So much pain. What should I do with the kids today? Maybe I'll take the big ones to the movies. So much pain. A coffee would be great after this sit. Wait, can I drink coffee while dealing with kidney stones? Pain. What is the name of that Beyoncé song? Pain. Just let it all go. Smile. I do this practice on behalf of all beings. Maybe I'll fast until dinner, too many carbs these past few days. Pain. May all beings be well in this moment. Pain. Just let it all go....*

I come back to my breath, my body, sounds. I rest and just let it all be. All of it—the pain, the thoughts, the emotions, the neutrality, the stability, the sounds—all of it is just passing through. Where could a single, enduring self abide in such a dynamic experience? I could easily say "I am in neutrality," just as I could say "I am in pain." Both are true. Both realities exist simultaneously, in different spaces within one space.

The pain in my body is the violent whipping winds and lightning of the tropical storm. My thoughts are the fluttering twists of the oak leaves. My arms and legs are the stability and strength of the tree trunks. Underneath it all, we are the same. The outside is the inside, the inside the outside.

When I look out, I see myself; when I look in, I see the landscape.

There really is no "me" here, none I can find today. The pain in my lower back feels deceptively constant, but when I rest my awareness on it, it crackles in and out like a lightbulb about to die, flaring with intensity and then dissipating into a dull, orange glow: impermanence. Thoughts pass through the sky of my mind like clouds, the pulse of wanting and not wanting creates tightness in my head that, met with loving awareness, dissipates.

It all comes and goes. Every thought, every sensation, every experience, is an inheritance from a lineage beyond time. This life, "my" life, is an expression of *sunyata*—emptiness. My existence is the activity of sunyata: the ceaseless flow of endless energies intertwined, rising and falling in different shapes, forms, and expressions. "I" is another way of describing the free nature of the universe that expresses itself in this very moment. In this "I" is the story of the entire universe. Awareness watches and smiles, nothing much to do but be present for it. When meditating, Suzuki Roshi says, we simply sit and observe the universal activity. This is enough. "I" am enough.

CHAPTER SIXTEEN

sit with my crew
stare at the wall
body is settled in posture
still this is practice
not a professional
may be monastic imposter
what does it matter
I'm not an actor
I try to silence the chatter
mind is so active
and it's reactive
Jackson Pollock with the splatter

# Such-
# ness

feeling my body
connect to my cushion
supported by earth underneath me
pray for the moment to teach me
feels like it hides when it sees me
every new breath is a season
fertile ground to put the seed in
pray that it grows to a tree
but my teacher said
I should let go of achievement
so I'm just sitting and letting go
dropping my body like Jericho
sound of the trumpet
is silent discussions as
breezes rush over the marigolds
as is above so is there below
85 necklaces herringbone
what this all is
we can barely know
nowhere to hide and
nowhere to go
sit and just notice and let it go
sit and just notice and let it go
sit and just notice and let it go
sit and just notice and let it go

shoulders relaxing
moments are passing
all in an orderly fashion
feeling the glow and I'm baskin'
but here comes a total distraction
here comes a thought I don't want to think
poison I really don't want to drink
here comes a feeling I hate to feel
take my illusions and make it real
I try to watch it and not react
inside I'm stumbling falling back
that's just anxiety talking trash
but sometimes it feels like a heart attack
show myself love as I watch it rise

show myself love as I watch it stay
show myself love as I watch it fade
show myself love as I watch it change
compassion for self
back to the body and breath
and the sounds all around me
sit and let gravity ground me
the moment was lost
but it found me
started out seeking enlightenment
putting my feet in the tiger's den
'til I realized I'm already free
and freedom itself is already me
feel my whole life in a silent sit
peace is so deep
I could die like this
freedom so spacious
could fly like this
anxiety's back
I just smile at it
feel my whole life in a silent sit
peace is so deep
I'm alive in it
freedom so spacious
could fly like this
joy in my heart
and I smile at it
loving it all then letting go
loving it all then letting go
loving it all then letting go
loving it all then letting go

# CHAPTER SEVENTEEN

# Frozen Lake

letting go gives us freedom
and freedom
is the only condition for happiness
if in our hearts, we still cling to anything
anger, anxiety, or possessions
we cannot be free.

sitting at the edge of a frozen lake
I come to realize the universe makes no mistakes
water bubbles suspended in time
edge of the water
looking at the edge of my mind
watching the motion pictures that flicker
behind my eyelids I'm wondering why my vision
makes everything look divided
got memories of the sky
as an eagle when I was flying
connected by the thread of the essence
that lives inside us
I'm empty
but I'm full
I'm on fire
but I'm cool
compassion made me a teacher
desire made me a fool (uh)
self-hatred makes me question what my purpose is
I R.ecognize A.ccept it I.nvestigate and I N.urture it[3]
when everything's connected remember
then I forget it I'ma die a living legend
remember that and respect it
life is what you make it it's never what you expected
let go of the past and future forever live in the present

my joy is like spring, so warm
it makes flowers bloom all over the Earth
my pain is like a river of tears,
so vast it fills the four oceans.

please call me by my true names,
so I can hear all my cries and my laughter at once,
so I can see that my joy and pain are one

I remember holding my mother's hand
while she's chanting the Lotus Sutra
it didn't make sense to me
but at least I was closer to her
*nam myoho renge kyo*
maintain pure
devotion to the bodhisattva path
holding contraband as I got older
started letting go of holding mother's hand
selling drugs and using drugs and sex just to become a man
wish I knew then what I know now
how could I understand
I had to reach the end of self-loathing
to find where love began
meditate in the shadows of Buddha statues and candles
watching how intrusive thoughts maneuver
and then attack you
delusion is laughing at you
confusion clapping back at you
it's precisely these illusions you're gonna have to unravel
sit down
breathe quietly
show love to your anxiety
everything is changing
you can use your inner eye to see
the higher me is looking at the lower me inside of me
the more I look the more I see that no one is inside

except earth, fire, water, and wind
moving together and freedom is my true nature
I'm in this moment forever
until I really get it
I'll do my best to remember
compassion for me and you
while I keep my mind in the present
life is what you make it it's never what you expected
I sat at the frozen water
and looked at what it reflected

maybe it's all just a dream
in between silence and screams
I want to know what it means
for my heart to be free
so I'm a man I'm a child
traveling mile after mile
searching below
and above
riding the wings of a dove

the rhythm of my heart is the birth and death
of all that is alive
please call me by my true names,
so I can hear all my cries and my laughter at once,
so I can see that my joy and pain are one
Clear reflective light, meeting spring, one action

³ This line references the Insight Meditation practice of RAIN, developed by
Michele McDonald, popularized by Tara Brach, and taught to me by Bhante
Buddharakkita. RAIN is a system of mindful attention and care for strong
emotional states. We RECOGNIZE our emotion(s) with kind, nonjudgmental
awareness; ACCEPT them as they are, not pushing them away or holding onto
them tightly; INVESTIGATE them, noticing their qualities, where they reside
in the body, their shape, color, texture, what the emotion is believing; and
NURTURE them by offering loving kindness to ourselves and to the emotion
specifically, either physically by placing a hand over the heart or abdomen
or subtly by sending waves of loving energy to the place we need it most.

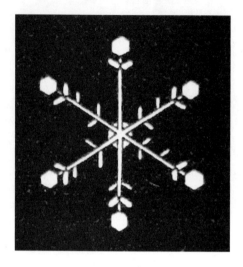

and development of my album *AMIDA* took place while I taught meditation retreats. Retreat settings are typically surrounded by nature, and I feel nature is a co-writer of this entire album. I believe everything on earth is nature, even man-made things, so I need to make a distinction here: the type of nature I'm referring to is the nature that is trees, wild animals, and bodies of water, not necessarily the nature that is cars and skyscrapers.

I wrote "Frozen Lake" at Prindle Pond Retreat Center in Massachusetts, where I co-taught a New Year's meditation retreat for teenagers. During my downtime, I explored the land around the center, enchanted by the energy of naked trees and stoic pines in the New England winter. One day as I walked, I stumbled upon a vast lake, its surface completely frozen. You could stand on it! I had never seen or experienced such a thing, and I was fascinated. Tiny bubbles of air trapped in the ice, billions of micro exhalations from the lake's last breaths before freezing, appeared as galaxies of stars in a universe under my feet. Crows cawed overhead, their call reminding me of my grandmother, now an ancestor (whose tribal symbol is the crow), and my connection to all things. The lake was silent in the way frozen things are, but it also moved slightly when you stood on it, reminding you of its depth.

Teenage years are difficult for many families, and ours was no exception. When my wife and I had Samadhi, we were very young parents. I wasn't always skillful in my parenting, didn't always see the ways I repeated harmful patterns I had experienced in my own childhood. I thought of myself as a liberal parent, since I didn't subject my children to the kind of strict regime I sometimes experienced as a kid. But just as the eye cannot see itself, I didn't realize I unwittingly perpetuated some behaviors—yelling, domineering, shaming, threatening—I had vowed to leave behind me. As I grew in my practice and in my parenting, I learned to parent in a more gentle, nuanced way. Still, the impacts of those earlier times remained.

Entering her teenage years, Samadhi developed a distinct sense of self and, reflecting on her childhood, grew distant from me. Not fully understanding why at first but feeling shame once comprehension dawned, I grew distant as well and exacerbated the natural separation that happens between parents and teens. It was a painful time. Samadhi and I had barely spoken the winter and spring the year before this New Year's retreat, and by the time I went to Plum Village the previous summer, we weren't speaking at all. Things between us were silent in the way frozen things are. I surrendered to the distance, but I thought about Samadhi a lot while I was in Plum Village. I thought about my own childhood, my own suffering, and how I had at times parented out of fear, anxiety, and anger in ways I had vowed not to. Feeling shame, sadness, and hopelessness, I cried often.

At first, I cried for our relationship and out of grief, but then my tears began to transform. One day I spoke with Brother Phap Lai, who shared a practice of healing our inner child. He guided me to visualize myself as the

# Things between us were silent in the way frozen things are.

child I once was, in a moment when I needed support or safety, and to offer myself what I had needed at that time. As a more skillful adult, he told me, I had the power to offer healing support to my inner child. Soon, the tears I cried were for the child within me who still suffered, who I could now connect with and offer love and support to.

I remembered my own early introduction to the Dharma. My mother became a practicing Buddhist in the Nichiren tradition when I was very young, and I wondered what had drawn her, a Ghanaian immigrant in the 1980s, to a tradition that seemed very different from the Akan tribal and colonizing Christian traditions she knew. I speculated that maybe she was inspired by artists like Tina Turner, Herbie Hancock, Wayne Shorter, and John and Alice

Coltrane—Black musicians who had embraced the teachings of the Buddha or the philosophies of the East. But when I asked her years later, the answer was much simpler: "I was looking for peace of mind," she said. "A Nichiren priest happened to approach a friend and me with a pamphlet about Buddhism, and we decided to check out the temple. As soon as I entered, I knew it was the right place for me. Buddhism is the path of turning poison into medicine."

The sense of ease, joy, and safety I felt and still feel when I'm with my mother is a refuge hard to describe. As an only child, it was easy for me to go wherever she went—to the grocery store, on a business trip, or to the Japanese Buddhist temple in nearby Silver Spring, Maryland.

# when we take care of ourselves, we do so on behalf of all beings, for all time.

Visiting the temple with my mother and experiencing the chanting, lighting of incense, and bowing, all of it seemed so magical and profound to me as a child. As I got older, similar sites flashed across the TV screen: "Black Belt Theater" on Saturday morning public-access television showed martial arts heroes receiving blessings at the temple before facing their adversaries or avenging their masters. Perhaps chanting, lighting incense, and bowing were the activities of heroes, I thought. As I grew older and entered adolescence, those teen years arrived for our family—the safety my mother provided grew thinner, though not for her lack of trying. The epidemic of drugs and violence sweeping the nation in the early 90s reached me, as did the glorification of crime and hypersexuality in popular culture. Combined with my desire to fit in, to not feel so alone, and to find a place in the world, I drifted away from my mother's care and protection. I tried to embody what I thought it meant to be strong. The sense of isolation I felt in my youth, partly due to experiencing sexual assault when I was very young and near-constant bullying in school, motivated me to decide I would no longer be a victim. Trying to unskillfully armor myself against pain brought on immense turmoil and self-loathing, which eventually impacted my own parenting.

Thầy says when we take care of ourselves, we do so on behalf of all beings, for all time. Our ancestors, from the beginning of time to now, are within our minds and bodies here in the present, and all who will come after us until the end of time are also here in our minds and bodies right now. When we heal ourselves, we give our parents and our ancestors opportunities to heal, and we do the same for our children. I spent many days and nights walking the grounds of Plum Village, offering love and healing to my inner child and compassion to the young parent I was when generational patterns subtly and easily defied my best intentions.

Months passed. On the surface, not much changed. Samadhi and I still were not speaking much, but when we did, our words were chosen carefully and kindly. Both of us were working on ourselves, that much was clear. By the time the new year rolled around, she expressed interest in attending the retreat I was scheduled to teach at Prindle Pond. Samadhi deciding to join this New Year's retreat was a landmark in our father-daughter relationship (which had

become strained, to say the least). She had been going to meditation classes and retreats all her life, first as a child attending offerings I led before losing interest as a young teen and later rediscovering meditation as an older teen choosing to go on retreats.

The retreat at Prindle was a space of gradual healing for Samadhi and me, both personally (speaking for myself) and collectively. As I sat at the edge of the frozen lake and experienced the movement of stillness, I looked at my own journey as a practitioner, a child, and a human. I looked at the distance between my intellectual understanding of the spiritual path and my everyday experience of life. At the edge of this frozen lake, I allowed my whole life to be present:

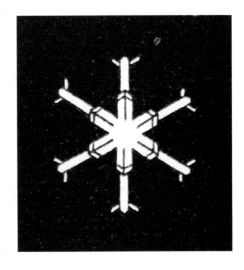

the parts that were open and free like the sky above and the birds flying through it as well as the parts that were still frozen—my mental health challenges, my unhealthy habits, my trauma. Each moment was a mixture of pain, exhilaration, and wakefulness, like feeling a gust of winter air. "Frozen Lake" is a song about human struggles, ineffability, and healing along the liberative path of Dharma.

Any practice of relating to our lives with presence and kindness can be a source of deep healing. I felt this process at work in the reconciliation between my daughter and me. For Samadhi's decision to come to the retreat, for the many talks we had afterward, for the time we spent together, just the two of us in quarantine right after the retreat—watching anime, remembering each other, being brand new, beginning anew—and for her being a part of this song: for all of these things, I am humbled and grateful beyond measure.

But it all led me back to the path, to the Dharma, to self-compassion and presence, to making this song. I looked at both what was frozen within me and what was warm, open, and free. Only in the warmth of kind awareness can the icicles of trauma melt into waters of freedom. Healing and transformation are lifelong journeys—at least they have been for me. There really is no escape from pain. As Thầy says, "The way out is in."

Within each one of us is the full spectrum of human possibility, from murderer to enlightened sage. Remembering this gives me a sense of both humility and hope: all realities are present in this mind and body. What I choose to nurture and cultivate is what takes root, grows, blooms, and ultimately falls to nourish the soil for what comes next. Thầy's poem, "Call Me By My True Names," speaks to this so powerfully. On "Frozen Lake," Samadhi reads Thầy's words:

*the rhythm of my heart is the birth and death of all that is alive.*
*please call me by my true names,*
*so I can hear all my cries and my laughter at once,*
*so I can see that my joy and pain are one.*

●

# CHAPTER EIGHTEEN

# Sasana

## (To My Children)

dear Sundara, Samadhi, Sati-Ananda and Siddhattha
this is me, your father
now, I don't know if I'm the guy
you woulda chose
if you had full control
but that's just how it goes
and this is a song
to let you know
the feelings that are there
even though no words
could ever really compare

I don't know how
to put in words
all that I feel
all I've observed
all that you've taught
all that I've learned
all I've awakened to
since you've returned
all of the love
all of the tears
all of the confidence
all of the fears
all happiness
all of the pride
all of the ignorance I try to hide
all your accomplishments
all of your glory
all the new chapters you write in your story
all of the patience
all the devotion

all of the beautiful, painful emotions
all the success
all of the failure
sometimes I can't believe
half of me made ya
but sometimes I can
look at your hands
look at your art
look at your spark
thank you for life
thank you for hope
thank you for giving me reasons to cope
thank you for laughter
thank you for lessons
thank you for thousands and billions of blessings
thank you for sharing
thank you for speaking
thank you for even the secrets you're keeping
you are the Buddhas, the Bodhis
the true and the holy
you love me even though you know me
and my imperfections
I try to correct them and be your example
and be your protection
bring me your problems
your sorrows, your questions
we'll figure out some way to solve them together
I will accept you, I will defend you
if I don't know something I won't pretend to

life is a gift
nothing is permanent
live in the moment
absorb it and learn from it
take what you've learned and apply it with kindness
and know that your spirit's already enlightened
cherish existence
know what your worth is
whatever brings you the most joy
is your purpose
nobody else is in your mind but yourself
so only you can truly be kind to yourself
there is no need
to free yourself
you are already free
just be yourself
love yourself for who you are
you will always be my shooting stars
daddy loves you
no surprise
I will always be by your side
in the morning
in the nighttime
I'll be there for you every lifetime
be there for each other
take care of each other
and remember
no one can compare
to your mother

# CHAPTER NINETEEN

I been switching lanes with the shit
came into the game with a brick
had to break it down into pieces
Leonardo
Mona Lisas
I just want to fly with the Birds
surf on the tide when it curves
some will get rich or die tryin'
but I don't wanna die unenlightened

# Un-
# enlight-
# ened

pose for the lights in the cameras
third eye blind from the scanners
fourth eye woke on the crown though
what goes around comes around bro
Bel Pre Road from the ground floor
even though I'm always out of town, Lord
deep breath deep feel rise and the fall
just like suicides on the doors
but I don't wanna die anymore

I just wanna arrive at the shore
wouldn't wish my pain or nobody else
but the only one to
blame is my fucking self
break one link and it falls
apart
take your broken heart and
you call it art
learn one thing from your
man Born
from a seed to a lotus you can transform

I been switching lanes ...
but I don't wanna die unenlightened

when I was a child I was so young
got a little older I was so sprung
now that I'm a man I'm like ho hum
puttin' new raps over old drums
don't be so eager to grow up

just slow up
you grow up a little too fast and you know what
this whole game is ruthless
its run by computers
the algorithm determines what your mood is
my mood is my mudra
my watch is my chakra
rising kundalini in white Lamborghini
it's starts with your
breathing the mantra repeating
that I am enough
flip the tarot for reading
it reads that each moment is just what you make it
wisdom and compassion
is how you awaken
PSA from your man Born
from a seed to a lotus you can transform

I been switching lanes...
but I don't wanna die unenlightened

I been sit in meditation every day now
from the morning to the time that I lay down
hop out the coupe and hop right in the booth
and I hope what I write can inspire the youth eh
pray now spread love every day now
I remember bus rides on the greyhound
told my fam I'll be down if you stay down
Tommy boy why'd you have to go away now
if you really think about it
all we need is to be present
with love and justice
but the system can't trust it
so sad that sometimes
I can't discuss it
bust it
so I look at my mind
and try to figure out
a way put myself in the dirt
so I can dig us out
I chose a different route
I'm sitting down and breathing deep
just to receive a way to help all of my niggas out
homie where did the day go day go
too much of the yayo yayo
turn your brain into play-doh play-doh
okay big bro if you say so
we just hiding our pain
what's the point of it all
if we dying in vain
take a ride in my lane
what's the source of the
spark that ignited the flame

I been switching lanes...
but I don't wanna die unenlightened

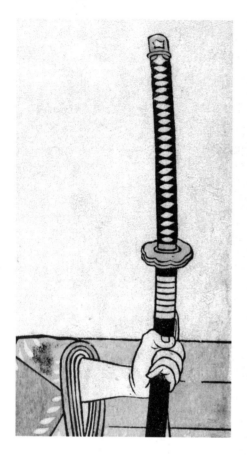

but not before they murder his wife. Together with his young son, Daigoro, Ogami walks the path of bloody revenge. As he travels the Japanese countryside with his son in search of those who wronged him, the two get into many adventures helping those in need along the way. Together, they become the titular *Lone Wolf and Cub*.

My own awareness of *LWAC* began when I first heard the classic hip-hop album *Liquid Swordz* by The GZA of Wu-Tang Clan as a teenager. Several skits on the album sample the English-dubbed version of *Lone Wolf and Cub*, and over the years I became a huge fan of both the film series and the manga. There's something particularly compelling about the juxtaposition of vulnerable and invulnerable, innocent and guilty, young and old, and how the lines between the two are often blurred over the course of our lives and experiences.

"Unenlightened" is written from the perspective of the warrior. It's written from experience. I've been on both sides of the fence, switching lanes between light and dark, and I've found what matters most to me: realizing my full potential, waking up from my illusions.

In Buddhism, the cycle of *samsara* (the endless round of suffering through

for "Unenlightened," written by me and directed by my friend Tim Shelby, is part Buddhist allegory, part nod to the Black samurai, Yasuke, and part homage to the samurai manga and film series *Lone Wolf and Cub (LWAC)*. *LWAC* is an epic samurai story of betrayal and revenge. It tells the tale of Ogami Ittō, a prominent samurai betrayed by the shogun because of his indomitable skill with the sword. When the shogun sends ninjas to assassinate Ogami, Ogami thwarts their attack,

The music video

birth and death lifetime after lifetime) is spun by the three poisons of greed, hatred, and delusion. Because of our ignorance of how we and the world around us truly are, we relate to reality in a way that is incongruent with its actual nature. We crave permanence where there is none, fear loss when loss is inevitable, and regard change as misfortune though it is fundamental to life. We find it hard to relax into the flow of existence—we neglect to see life as the wonderful, majestic, temporary miracle it is and instead treat it as something that should last forever, never harm us, and only change in our favor. Thus, we suffer and cause suffering for others. Thích Nhất Hạnh famously said, "Man is not our enemy ... our enemies are anger, hatred, ignorance, and fear."

In the video for "Unenlightened," I wanted to explore the spiritual path from the perspective of a warrior traveling with a child. The incredible story of Yasuke, the Black man who became a Samurai in feudal Japan, was also a source of inspiration. I cast myself as the unnamed Warrior (Lone Wolf/Yasuke) and my son, Siddhattha, or Siddha for short, as the Child (cub). Warrior is a seeker on the spiritual path who has done his best to practice the way but has been harmed and caused harm in the course of his life. He is hardened. Child represents the inner child of Warrior: his heart, his compassion, and that which is still good and innocent—within him and within all living beings. In the music video for "Unenlightened," Warrior and Child are not on a mission of revenge, but of enlightenment. Warrior seeks to defeat all that stands between himself and full awakening and to bring Child with him. Along the way, they are attacked by three devils: Greed, Hatred, and Delusion.

Referencing the violence of the original *Lone Wolf and Cub*, Warrior draws his sword and engages the devils in mortal combat each time he encounters them. In three separate battles, Warrior strikes down each of the devils, sometimes with telepathic assistance from Child. As Warrior and Child escape, the camera pans over the bodies of the fallen devils to see the seemingly dead rivals revive, their eyes popping back open and their bodies rising from the ground to pursue the warrior again. In the final ambush, greed, hatred, and delusion attack Warrior and Child together. As they approach, Warrior and Child stumble upon Wisdom, a beautiful Black goddess in African garb (played by my wife, Ayanna). Wisdom stands next to Warrior and Child as they face down the three ominously approaching devils. Warrior draws his sword, and even Child raises a hand, ready to engage in the violence Warrior has conditioned him to believe is viable. But Wisdom places her hands on the lone wolf and cub, encouraging them to sit in meditation and allow the devils to approach. They comply, surrendering to their fate. Warrior and Child sit with Wisdom; Greed, Hatred, and Delusion tower over them. As Warrior accepts these devils for what they are, the three letters YAE (you are enough) appear on his forehead and the foreheads of his companions. Wisdom, Warrior, and Child open their eyes to see the devils have vanished, leaving behind a clear blue sky and a garden of flowers.

The video for "Unenlightened" is a reflection of much of my own spiritual practice. In the early days of my meditation practice, I made the mistake of viewing the expressions of my own ignorance, the echoes of my trauma, and the manifestations of my karma—my own greed, hatred, and delusion—as enemies to be vanquished. Reading the hagiographies of great meditation masters like Ajahn Mun and Ajahn Chah who sat deep in the jungles of Thailand and did battle with their *kilesas* (spiritual defilements), watching films about great Zen masters who sat against walls of ice to prevent themselves from falling asleep during meditation, and

# Paradoxically, this is true fearlessness, true warriorship: to lay down one's arms and offer what will truly be of benefit, even one's own self.

reflecting on the story of Siddhartha (the historical Buddha) meeting Mara and vanquishing ignorance as well as death itself made me feel I needed to go to the depths of extreme spiritual heroism in my own life and practice.

I felt I needed to use my meditation practice to destroy all that was "wrong" with and within me. I turned my meditation cushion into a battlefield where I slashed at my anxieties, intrusive thoughts, and fears with the swords of judgment, disgust, and shame. The casualties were my mental, physical, and emotional health. I look back on this version of

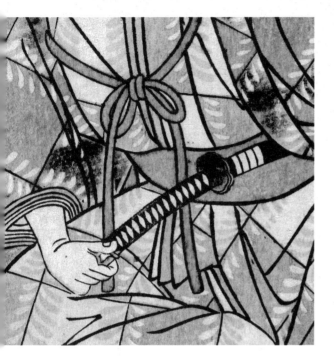

benefit, even one's own self. This is the ultimate expression of the warrior spirit. When we look for the roots of greed, hatred, and delusion, we find our wrong perceptions and our misunderstanding of who we really are and what reality is. Seeing clearly, we say to our demons, "Whatever you need to heal, to be pacified, may I become that thing. I offer myself to you as that." Using our creativity, informed by love and understanding, we pacify that which torments us. In this surrender, we don't die. We don't lose anything except our fear and wrong perceptions.

I want to give a special shout-out to my son, Siddha, who was five years old when we filmed this video in the hot August sun over the course of many days. He truly embodied the elements of the story we were trying to tell, seeming to perfectly understand his role in everything despite his young age. It's a true joy to work with my family and friends in spiritually creative ways. I am forever grateful.

myself with a lot of compassion—he wanted so badly to be good. I wish I had understood my experience as symptoms of mental health conditions that needed more care than vipassana meditation alone could provide; I needed a softer approach to spiritual practice, one that included self-compassion, mindfulness, and therapy.

In the video for "Unenlightened," the three devils are only overcome when Warrior, accompanied by Wisdom, surrenders and offers himself to them. Paradoxically, this is true fearlessness, true warriorship: to lay down one's arms and offer what will truly be of

●

you see me fly when I'm writin'
this is that G&D moment
call it the rise of the titans
picture perspectives of paragraphs
preaching power persistently
who vanished from the world 'n
returned shrouded in mystery
a dreamer for real
what I think 'n I feel
these darker forces they close in
'n plot 'n scheme on my skill
when I'm in front of the lord
and all my secrets revealed
will I discover repentance
after I bleed and heal
I meditate on the meanin'
feelin' awake when I'm dreaming
evening I'm basically healin'
from conversations with demons
police is slangin' them bullets
first they aim 'n then pull it
then they claim he deserve it
'cause his sweater was hooded
I put it all in a journal
ain't got no one to turn to
callin' me Dante Alighieri
as I learn this inferno
I'm just a scholar with dollars
all my daughters is wearin' Prada
none if any can stop us
they just follow after we pop up
I'm a mafia don
pray for peace in my soul
satan will chop at ya fingers
soon as you reachin' your goal
none of my niggas is scared
we came equipped and prepared

# Joshua

this is that unspoken feeling
you can feel in the air
you see my mother was Buddhist
and my father was genius
and I was studying bibles because my idol
was Jesus
I put it all in together
between that fall and December
and made a path of my own
man that's all I remember
you can judge if you want
but I'm just being a man
I can't ignore the composition
of my DNA strand
first everybody was doubting
now they kiss on the ring
I guess I needed it to balance
my position as king
I'm drinkin' vodka with poets
rollin' ganja with doctors
writin' the spirit of my people
I'm a conduit author
so many great but don't know it
so they wait for the moment
but a real boss knows
you gotta take it and own it
look for a theme in my verses
its Lamborghinis and churches
and risin' up from the bottom
when you feel like you worthless
so many nights I remember
I just wanted to end it
I awoke the next morning feelin' like I resurrected
these second chances was given

I could master the mission
finding freedom of the spirit
in the land of the living
pray what we learning can heal us
and that the journey complete us
and if I burn along the way
may I return like the Phoenix

my email. A producer friend of mine has sent new music for me to listen to. I listen. The energy of the beat enters my body in waves. There's an immediate attraction, then comes infatuation, then falling in love. I envision a future with this music, a future where our energies intertwine and become a song. I am in divine love. The Holy Spirit drops into me. The Source enters. I start to speak in tongues, uttering gibberish to the rhythm of the music, imaginary words with feelings but not yet meaning. There's an intensity in my chest, a warm, compelling, electric hum, an invisible cord plugged into an unseen power. I am alive.

I ache, words and ideas form in my heart and body. Too much, too many, I'm engorged. It hurts. I can't breathe. Things begin to happen outside my control. My fingers tremble as I whisper words that match the rhythm of the Pentecostal gibberish from before. My hands tingle and pulse with excitement as I write the words. I'm channeling. I'm possessed. It's not me anymore. I'm the host.

Words undam themselves and pour through my body—my brain, my heart, my mouth, my hands. Memories, feelings, ambitions, heartbreaks, insights, failures, victories, desires, defiances, and prayers rocket their way through my being and I vomit them out in an excruciating, rhyming ecstasy. I could die right now.

My breathing deepens as, against the wishes of the source, I pause. I breathe. I breathe. I breathe. I read aloud what has been written so far. I take the reins and make adjustments, find better words to express the intention of the Source. I adjust patterns of delivery, I employ invisible mathematics to create verbal fractals. I do this in reverence to the Source.

Then I become hijacked again—the Source plugs the cord back in and I am repossessed. We wrestle for control. I let go, I surrender. The intensity resumes, but there is also freedom and joy mixed with an electric, compelling ache. I'm on fire. I'm flying. I surrender. There is trust between us now. I open freely as the Source pours information and energy into my being, collecting the raw material from all life and my own life in particular, turning it into rhymes. Then the source relents, giving me space to fashion the words with the skills my ancestors gave me. Even as I assume control, there is no self at the wheel. It is the virtues, laws, and powers of all who came before me, all that is around me, and all that will be that allow me to carve the words

into detailed form. Awareness is my witness.

It's time to land the ship. It's time to write the last words of the song. This song doesn't require any breaks, refrains, or hooks. It is an entire download from within and without. As Thầy reminds me, these distinctions—"outside, inside"—don't exist at all.

This song is a bodhisattva prayer. The source and I sit together and recite our prayer again and again. We are proud parents of a new song. We name him "Joshua."

# Ana-panasati

# CHAPTER TWENTY-ONE

*Translations (from the Pali)

*Ānāpānasati:* mindfulness of the breath

*Satipaṭṭhāna:* The Four Foundations of Mindfulness
(body, feelings, mind, phenomena)

*Mettā:* lovingkindness

*Karuṇā:* compassion

*Muditā:* sympathetic joy

*Upekkhā:* equanimity

in the morning
anapanasati
won't you take me
to old satipatthana
In the mid-day
metta and karuna
in the nighttime
mudita and upekkha
tell me mama,
will you live forever?
tell me father,
that you'll always be here,
tell me lover,
are you really with me?
tell me sweet child,
that I have nothing to fear

I don't know what I want to say on this
maybe I'll pray on this
may I be a doctor and medicine
for the sick
may I help the people navigate
when they're taking a trip
may I be a light in the shadows
so they can see
may I help them to remember
that they are already free
what's a flight without some turbulence?
maybe it's all designed
to point the heart to what its purpose is

in the morning
anapanasati...

a cloud never perishes
when you see the rainfall
you can feel the evidence
a cloud never perishes
when you see the frozen lake
you can feel the evidence
a cloud never perishes
river to the ocean
you can feel the evidence
a cloud never perishes
when you see my tears fall
you can see the evidence

in the morning
anapanasati...

I can't be mad at my fate
a sink full of dishes means my family ate
margielas in the grocery
oatmeal and cherry preserves
my mind is the verse
shadow self
that's the reverb
how do I deal with these waves of emotions
combined with the joy and the pain of devotion
before I was born and my name wasn't spoken

I still existed as frameless and open
I'm just reading the sutra seeking
the teachings of Buddha
natural fever reducer
drinking Kevita kombucha
a Black Buddhist Johnny Cash
yeah, you call me that
spiritual army brat
I used to dream of suicide,
but I learned
to have compassion
for the person I saw
when I looked inside

In the morning
Anapanasati...

**I pour tea.**

The amber-saffron liquid fills the small glass cup on the mini altar in front of me. Steam rises from the cup and licks at the air before disappearing, drawing my attention to the oak tree outside my window—its deep green leaves flutter gently in the summer wind. Every so often, the oak brushes against its longtime companion, a mighty old pine tree to its right. I kneel, supported by two large, black *zafus* (meditation cushions) underneath me. My knees, shins, and feet rest gently on a soft, amber-saffron *zabuton* (floor mat). My hands rest in my lap.

I sit and sip my tea. The warmth greets my mustache before the liquid touches my lips. The smell of oolong tea is wonderful, worth savoring. I breathe gently, holding the round, hot, glass with two hands as I taste the tea's bitter, earthy, ozone-sweetness. The heat slowly waterfalls into my stomach. I close my eyes and enjoy.

My ears hear raindrops before my eyes see them fall. A heavy downpour arrives suddenly. I close my eyes again. Countless water droplets land on countless oak leaves and pine needles, sounding like applause. I open my eyes. The rain ends as suddenly as it began; the trees return to stillness, to silence, adorned now with water drops that glitter like diamond stars in the sun.

My hands come together in my lap, the left on top of the right. Slowly, I bring my thumbs together, forming the cosmic mudra. Police sirens blare. My body feels awake, integrating the tea. The water drops are already evaporating from the pine needles.

My body is full of sensations: ease in my legs, a relaxed heaviness in my arms, heat in my hands, small flashes of pain across my lower back like lightning at the end of a storm. My head feels surprisingly neutral—before my OCD treatment, I experienced so much pain and tension there. Gratitude blooms in my chest, spreading as an amber-saffron color through my torso and into my arms and legs.

A cardinal swoops and lands on an oak branch, reminding me of our two parakeets who died this month, Lapis and Peridot. This is the same window they perched on to look out at these same trees, the oak and the pine, season after season. *Lapis and Peridot are gone now*, I think to myself. A hollow, gray emptiness replaces the amber-saffron gratitude in my chest. *Everyone I love will die one day. I will die, my wife, my children, my parents, all of us are going to die. I've already lost so many friends....*

Car tires mix with wet pavement outside and create a peaceful hissing sound like soft waves. I feel my feet against the softness of the zabuton and my eyes find its partner-in-color, my cup of oolong tea, in front of a small, wooden statue of Thích Nhất Hạnh. *Thầy says death is an illusion.* My mind doesn't think this as much as my body feels it. The "dead" wood of a tree is now a beautiful statue of Thầy, reminding me death isn't real. The tea is the sky, the sun, the rain, the earth. So am I. I love you, Lapis and Peridot. I love you, Mom and Dad. I love you, Ayanna. I love you, Sundara, Samadhi, Sati, and Siddhattha. I love you, oak tree. I love you, pine tree. I love you, cardinal. I love you, zafu, zabuton, tea. I love you,

# Countless water droplets land on countless oak leaves and pine needles, sounding like applause.

body, mind, heart. I love you, Thầy. The sun announces itself through the oak leaves. I love you too, sun.

I am full and empty, happy and sad, endless and finite. I am pleasure, pain, and neutrality. I am one breath at a time. I am here, in this moment.

It's time to sit zazen. I lower my gaze and make peace with vastness.

●

# Acknowle -dgments

This book would not be possible without the love and patience of my wife and children and the guidance of my parents, parents-in-law, ancestors, Mother Nature, and my many Dharma teachers. I bow to you all with love, gratitude, and respect.

The songs referenced in this book could not exist without the producers, mixing and mastering engineers (special thank you to AJ Halpern), graphic designers, costume designers, and videographers who helped bring them to life.

To my chosen family—"The Rebels"—and to all of my friends and fellow musicians: my stories don't exist without you. I love you! To the entire Parallax Press staff—thank you for supporting this vision with such kindness, attention, and care. To my friend and manager Kristen Carranza, thank you for being by my side through this process. To my brother Tom Dern, I love you. I know you're still moving things around for me. Thank you, brother. We continue.

OFOSU JONES-QUARTEY is a meditation teacher, author, and musician hailing from the Washington, DC, area who is dedicated to sharing mindfulness, hip-hop, and self-compassion practices with the world. His live events are a hip-hop and meditation experience. Jones-Quartey leads meditation classes and retreats nationwide, having taught and led retreats at the Insight Meditation Community of Washington, the Insight Meditation Society (IMS), Spirit Rock, Brooklyn Zen Center, Cleveland Insight, and Inward Bound Mindfulness, among others. Jones-Quartey has also worked with schools and has co-written a mindfulness-based suicide prevention curriculum for teenagers as well as the children's books *You Are Enough* and *Love Your Amazing Self.*

As an accomplished hip-hop artist under the name "Born I," Jones-Quartey released the mindfulness-themed album *In This Moment* in 2021, earning a nomination for "Best Rap Album" at the Washington Area Music Awards (Wammies). In 2023, coinciding with the release of his second album, *AMIDA*—a spiritual, lo-fi hip-hop album exploring life, death, and Buddhist wisdom—Born I embarked on a music and meditation tour with the monks and nuns of Plum Village Monastery. In 2025, he released the album *Komorebi*—a minimalist, lyric-driven meditation on life, family, and spiritual practice.

Residing in Rockville, Maryland, with his wife and four children, Jones-Quartey continues to use creativity to guide individuals toward presence, stress reduction, and the cultivation of love and compassion for themselves and the world.

LINKS
bornimusic.com

CLASSES, EVENTS AND MORE
http://linktr.ee/bornimusic

ABOUT THE AUTHOR

TO HONOR

HIP-HOP'S

SPIRITUAL

POTENTIAL